Oxford International Primary

6

Maths

Student Book

Tony Cotton

Caroline Clissold

Linda Glithro

Cherri Moseley

Janet Rees

Language consultants:
John McMahon
Liz McMahon

OXFORD

Great Clarendon Street, Oxford, OX2 6DP, United Kingdom

Oxford University Press is a department of the University of Oxford. It furthers the University's objective of excellence in research, scholarship, and education by publishing worldwide. Oxford is a registered trade mark of Oxford University Press in the UK and in certain other countries.

British Library Cataloguing in Publication Data

Data available

ISBN 9781382006712

10 9 8 7

Paper used in the production of this book is a natural, recyclable product made from wood grown in sustainable forests. The manufacturing process conforms to the environmental regulations of the country of origin.

Printed in India by Multivista Global Pvt. Ltd

Acknowledgements

The publisher and authors would like to thank the following for permission to use photographs and other copyright material:

Cover artwork by Peskimo. **Photos: p17:** Kingppin/Shutterstock; **p20:** Christian Nieke/Shutterstock; **p94:** Africa Studio/Shutterstock; **p97:** MaraZe/Shutterstock; **p107:** entreguin/Shutterstock; **p122:** Paolo Gallo/Shutterstock; **p123:** Piotr Piatrouski/Shutterstock; **p124(t):** PhotoMavenStock/Shutterstock; **p124(m):** Oqbas/Shutterstock; **p125:** Volodymyr Burdiak/Shutterstock; **p138(bkgd):** Arnold OA Pinto/Shutterstock; **p138(br):** Rawpixel.com/Shutterstock; **p138(bl):** MarcelClemens/Shutterstock; **p138(ml):** Cls Graphics/Shutterstock; **p146:** StevanZZ/Shutterstock; **p147:** Amnat Phuthamrong/Shutterstock; **p171:** Stor24/Shutterstock; **p184:** Celso Pupo/Shutterstock; **p188(br):** AerialVision_it/Shutterstock; **p188(bl):** Samot/Shutterstock.

Artwork by Q2A Media Services Pvt. Ltd and Six Red Marbles.

Every effort has been made to contact copyright holders of material reproduced in this book. Any omissions will be rectified in subsequent printings if notice is given to the publisher.

Contents

How to use this book

The Student Book for *Oxford International Primary Maths* forms part of your mathematics lessons for this year. Your teacher will introduce the ideas through whole-class activities, then you will explore them in more depth using this book, before all coming back together to discuss what you have learned. Find out more at: www.oxfordprimary.com/international-maths

Structure of the book

This book is divided into 11 units. Each unit covers a different strand of mathematics.

What you will find in each unit

There are five types of lessons:

Engage introduces the unit's mathematical ideas.
It tells you what you will learn in the unit and includes the big question.

Discover introduces mathematical skills and concepts.

In **Explore** you practise the skills you learned in Discover.

Connect helps you make links between the different areas of mathematics in the unit.

In **Review** you show your teacher what you have learned in the unit.

What you will find in the lessons

Although each lesson is unique, they have common features:

Discover / **Explore** The lesson type tells you whether you are discovering new mathematical concepts or exploring concepts you have already been introduced to.

Key words
- equation
- variable

This box gives the key words for the lesson.

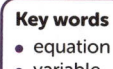 **Stretch zone** This challenges you to take your learning further.

In the speech bubbles, you will find useful hints, examples of how to complete a question, or extra questions to get you thinking about the mathematics you are doing.

Additional features

This shows you where you can practise the key vocabulary, either by writing the words or through a discussion.

This shows you where you can practise your mental maths skills such as your multiplication tables or other key number facts.

This shows you where you need to record your work in a notebook.

Glossary Key words are listed in a picture glossary at the end of the book. You can write your own definition for each word.

Teacher's Guide

The Teacher's Guide that accompanies this book provides lesson notes for each page.

Practice Book

At the bottom of each page in this book, there is a link to the Practice Book, where you can find extra practice to do in your lesson or at home.

1 Number and place value

?

How can I understand the value of very large numbers? How can I use large numbers and negative numbers?

Engage

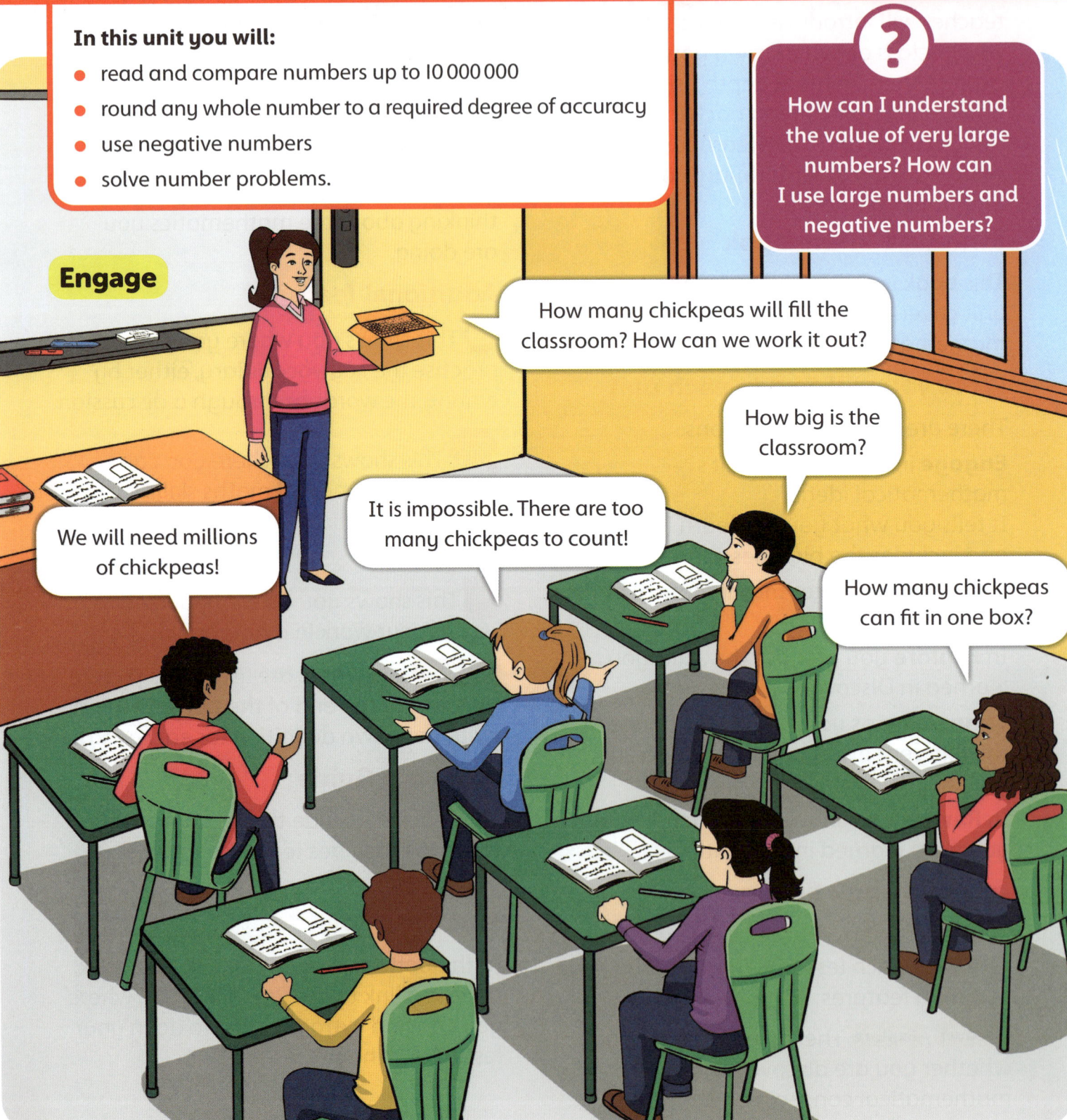

How many chickpeas will fill the classroom? How can we work it out?

How big is the classroom?

It is impossible. There are too many chickpeas to count!

We will need millions of chickpeas!

How many chickpeas can fit in one box?

1A Place value

Discover

Place-value game

Key words
- hundred thousand
- million
- ten million

| 0 | 1 | 2 | 3 | 4 |
| 5 | 6 | 7 | 8 | 9 |

1 Pick a card from a set of digit cards 0–9.

- Write the digit in any column in the top row of the place-value grid.

- Replace the card and repeat six more times. Now you will have a 7-digit number in the top row.

Repeat until all the rows are full.

Millions	Hundred thousands	Ten thousands	Thousands	Hundreds	Tens	Ones

Now complete these sentences about the numbers in the table.

2 The largest number is [   ].

The largest number possible using the digits from

this number is [   ].

3 The smallest number is [   ].

The smallest number possible using the digits from

this number is [   ].

4 The number nearest to 5 000 000 is [   ].

The number nearest to 5 000 000 using the digits from

this number is [   ].

You cannot change the position of any of your digits!

Stretch zone

What is the number nearest to 1 000 000 using the digits from **question 4**?
Explain how you know.

■ For more practice, go to Practice Book 6, page 15.

1A Place value

Explore

Multiply by 10, 100 and 1000

Use a calculator for this activity.

Key words
- place-value grid
- power of 10
- multiple of 10

1 Enter any 4-digit number into your calculator.

- Write the number in the first row of the place-value grid below.

Follow these instructions.

- Multiply the number by 10.
- Write the new number in the next row of the place-value grid.
- Multiply this new number by 10 two more times. Complete the next two rows of the table.

2 Repeat with a different 4-digit number.

What calculation is the same as multiplying by 10 twice?

	Millions	Hundred thousands	Ten thousands	Thousands	Hundreds	Tens	Ones
× 10							
× 10							
× 10							
× 10							
× 10							
× 10							

3 Now complete these sentences:

When you multiply by 10, the digits move ☐ place to the _____.

When you multiply by 100, _____

When you multiply by 1000, _____

Stretch zone

Can you write a general rule for multiplying a number by any power of 10?

8

1B Rounding

Discover

Round to the nearest 10, 100 and 1000

Pick four cards from a set of digit cards 0–9.

- Make ten different 4-digit numbers using these digits.
- Order the numbers from smallest to largest.
- Write the numbers in the first column of the table.
- Complete the other columns by rounding your numbers.

Worked example

Number	Round to the nearest 10	Round to the nearest 100	Round to the nearest 1000
5379	5380	5400	5000
7359	7360	7400	7000
9753	9750	9800	10 000

Number	Round to the nearest 10	Round to the nearest 100	Round to the nearest 1000

I picked these digits.

3 5 7 9

I can make 5379, 7359, 9753 and lots more.

I rounded each number to the nearest 10, 100 and 1000.

Remember: look at the digit to the right of the one you are rounding. If the digit is 5 or more, round up. If it is less than 5, round down.

 **Stretch zone**

I am thinking of a number. I round my number to 6000 to the nearest thousand. What is the smallest possible number I could be thinking of? What is the largest possible number?

■ For more practice, go to Practice Book 6, page 17.

Explore

Round and order numbers

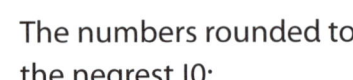

Key words
- round to the nearest
- 4-digit number

1 Pick four cards from a set of digit cards 0–9.

My four digits:

How do you know you have found all the possible numbers.

2 Use these digits to make as many different 4-digit numbers as you can. Write your numbers in the first box below.

3 Round all the numbers to the nearest 10. Write the rounded numbers in the second box.

All the possible numbers:

The numbers rounded to the nearest 10:

4 Use your rounded numbers to make correct number sentences.

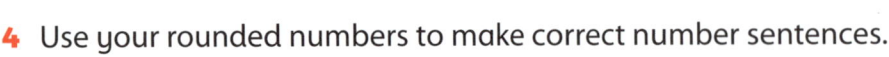

	<		<		<	
	>		>		>	
	<		<		<	
	>		>		>	
	<		<		<	
	>		>		>	

Explore (continued)

5 Choose eight of your original numbers from **question 2**.

- Label the ends of a number line with the correct thousands.
- Write the number in the correct place on the number line.

Worked example

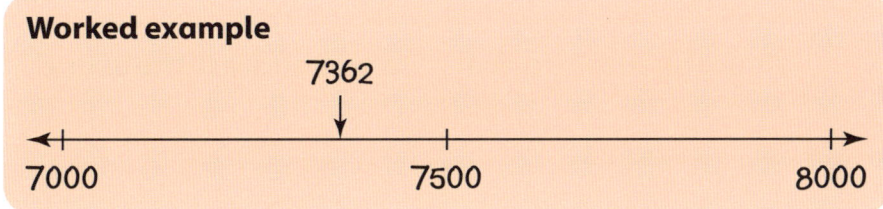

7362

7000   7500   8000

> I chose 7362. I labelled the number line with 7000 and 8000. I also labelled the halfway point to help me find the correct position.

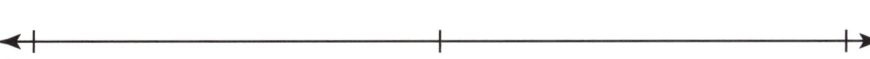

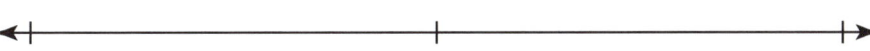

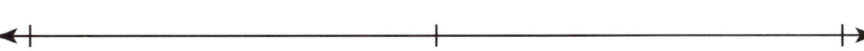

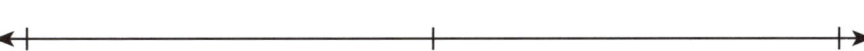

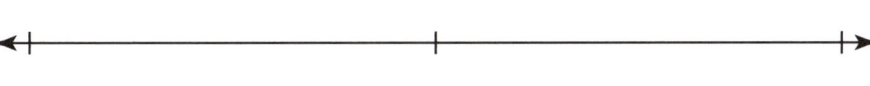

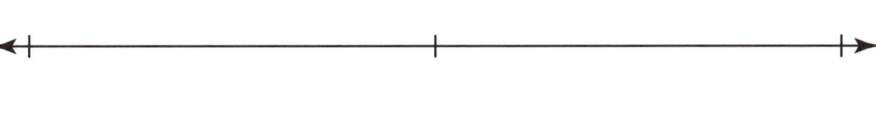

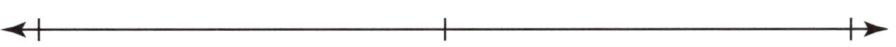

Explore (continued)

6 The table below shows supporter attendance numbers at seven English Premier League football clubs.

- Complete the table by rounding each number to the nearest thousand. The first one is done for you.

Football club		Average attendance	To the nearest thousand
Manchester United		74 528	75 000
Arsenal		59 079	
West Ham		58 336	
Tottenham Hotspur		54 130	
Manchester City		54 017	
Liverpool		52 731	
Newcastle United		51 515	

7 Calculate the following using the rounded numbers.

a The total attendance for these seven clubs

b The difference in attendance between Manchester United and Manchester City

c The difference in attendance between Liverpool and West Ham

d The difference in attendance between Arsenal and Tottenham Hotspur

Stretch zone

Find out about the attendance numbers at some sports clubs in your own country. Round the attendances to the nearest 100 or 1000 and order the clubs from largest attendance to smallest.

■ For more practice, go to Practice Book 6, page 18.

1C Using negative numbers

Discover

Positive and negative temperatures

I Draw lines to match the temperatures to the thermometers.

Key words
- temperature
- below freezing
- negative number

London 17°C   Moscow ⁻4°C   Oslo ⁻8°C   Bangkok 35°C   Dubai 42°C

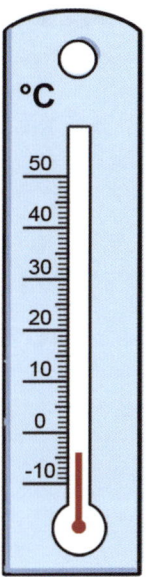 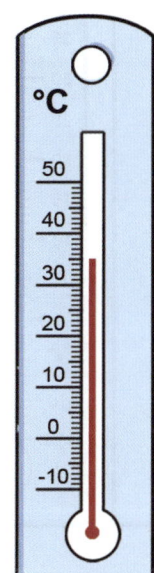 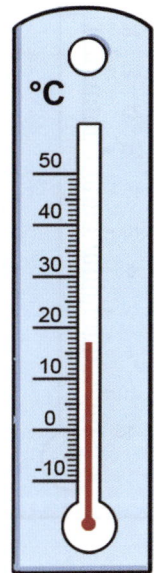 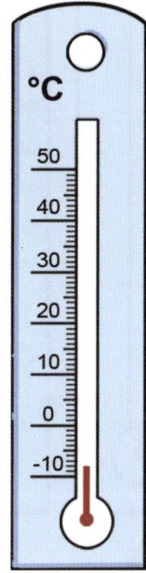 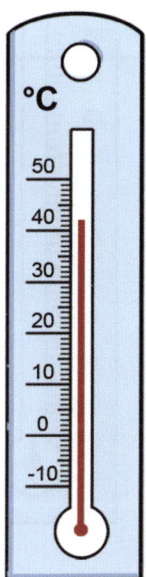

2 Look at the temperatures in the cities in **question** I.

- If you travel between the cities below, does the temperature rise or fall?
- What is the change in temperature?

a Bangkok to London   Rise / Fall

Change in temperature:  °C

b Bangkok to Dubai   Rise / Fall

Change in temperature:  °C

c Moscow to London   Rise / Fall

Change in temperature: °C

d Moscow to Oslo   Rise / Fall

Change in temperature:  °C

1 Number and place value

13

Discover (continued)

Try to find three positive temperatures and three temperatures below zero.

3 Choose six cities around the world. Use the internet to find the average temperature for each city in December.

● Draw the temperatures on the thermometers below.

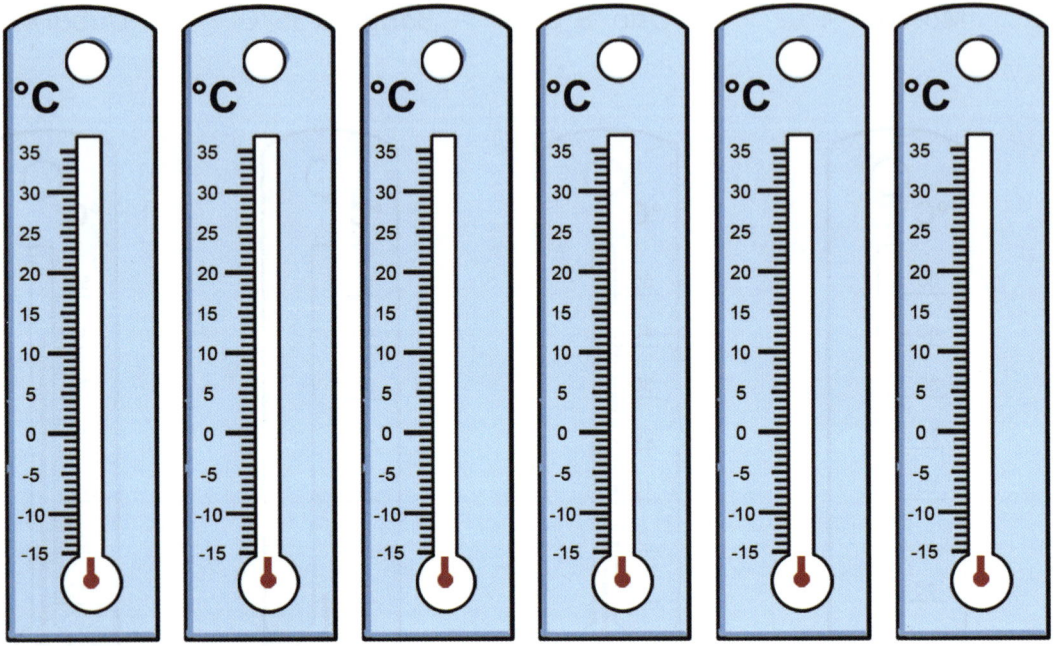

Stretch zone

Look at this table of temperatures in some cities around the world.

City	Temperature on Ist January	City	Temperature on Ist January
Anchorage		Sydney	28 °C
London	−2 °C	Harbin	
Oymyakon	−45 °C	Cairo	
Rio de Janeiro		Bangkok	

Use the following clues to complete the table.

● Cairo is 59 degrees warmer than Oymyakon.

● Rio de Janeiro is 38 degrees warmer than London.

● Harbin is 47 degrees colder than Sydney.

● Anchorage is 26 degrees colder than Cairo.

● Bangkok is 50 degrees warmer than Anchorage.

14

■ For more practice, go to Practice Book 6, page 19.

1C Using negative numbers

Explore

Negative number statements

Is each statement 'Always true', 'Sometimes true' or 'Never true'?
Circle the correct answer.

Key words
- negative number
- positive number

1

If you add two negative numbers, the answer is negative.

$$^-3 + {}^-2$$

Always true / Sometimes true / Never true

4

If you add a negative number and a positive number, the answer is positive.

$$^-3 + 6$$

Always true / Sometimes true / Never true

2

If you subtract a positive number from a negative number, the answer is positive.

$$^-7 - 9$$

Always true / Sometimes true / Never true

5

If you subtract a negative number from a negative number, the answer is negative.

$$^-4 - {}^-6$$

Always true / Sometimes true / Never true

3

If you subtract a positive number from a positive number, the answer is negative.

$$8 - 15$$

Always true / Sometimes true / Never true

6

If you subtract a negative number from a positive number, the answer is positive.

$$8 - {}^-6$$

Always true / Sometimes true / Never true

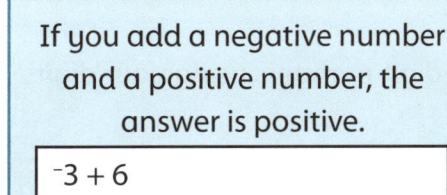

First do the calculation given for each statement. Then do at least two more calculations to see if you get the same results.

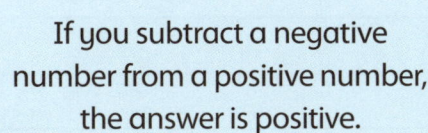

I did these calculations for the first statement:

$$^-3 + {}^-2 = {}^-5$$
$$^-10 + {}^-7 = {}^-17$$
$$^-4 + {}^-8 = {}^-12$$

All the answers are negative, so I think this statement is always true.

Stretch zone

Write calculations with these answers: 0, $^-13$ and 66. In each calculation, use any of the numbers $^-22$, $^-3$, 14, 39 and 88 and any combination of adding and subtracting.

1 Number and place value

15

■ For more practice, go to Practice Book 6, page 20.

1D Comparing numbers

Discover

Compare large numbers and negative numbers

Key words
- 7-digit number
- million
- hundred thousand
- negative number

1 Pick seven cards from a set of digit cards 0–9.

- Replace your card each time so it is possible to pick the same digit twice.
- Make nine different 7-digit numbers using your digits.

My numbers are:

I picked 1, 1, 2, 3, 5, 5, 6. The first two numbers I made were 1 561 235 and 5 235 611.

2 Write your numbers in the table, in order smallest to largest.

- Then write your numbers in words.

Number	Number in words

3 Use the same digits to make five 2-digit negative numbers.

- Write them in order, from smallest to largest.

Stretch zone

What is the difference between your smallest and largest negative numbers?
Write some negative number calculations for a partner to solve.

16

■ For more practice, go to Practice Book 6, page 21.

1D Comparing numbers

Explore

Compare populations and temperatures

1 Write the populations of these countries in order, starting with the smallest.

Key words
- 7-digit number
- million
- hundred thousand
- negative number

Iceland 356 991

Slovenia 2 078 938

Barbados 285 000

Uruguay 3 473 730

Bahrain 1 234 571

Brunei 393 162

Botswana 2 373 622

Tonga 103 036

2 Write the highest and lowest populations in words.

Highest: _____

_____

Lowest: _____

_____

3 These are the temperatures at which some substances solidify.

- Write the temperatures in order, starting with the lowest temperature.

Mercury ⁻39 °C   Ethanol ⁻114 °C   Water 0 °C   Carbon dioxide ⁻78 °C

Glycerol 18 °C   Lead 327 °C   Nitric acid ⁻42 °C   Sodium 98 °C

4 Write the highest and lowest solidifying temperatures in words.

Highest: _____

Lowest: _____

Stretch zone

Use the internet to find five substances with very low solidifying temperatures. Can you put these five temperatures in order?

■ For more practice, go to Practice Book 6, page 22.

1E Using place-value facts

Discover

Number pairs for 100, 10 and 1

Follow these steps five times and complete the table.

- Choose two cards from a set of digit cards 0–9.
- Make a 2-digit number. Use this number to make number pairs to 100, 10 and 1.
- Reverse the digits. Use this new number to make pairs to 100, 10 and 1.

Number	pair to 100	pair to 10	pair to 1

I picked 5 and 6 and made 56. Here are my pairs:

$$56 + 44 = 100$$
$$5.6 + 4.4 = 10$$
$$0.56 + 0.44 = 1$$

I reversed the digits to make 65.

$$65 + 35 = 100$$
$$6.5 + 3.5 = 10$$
$$0.65 + 0.35 = 1$$

Stretch zone

How does knowing pairs to 10 help you find pairs to 10 000?

Write some examples.

18

■ For more practice, go to Practice Book 6, page 23.

1E Using place-value facts

Explore

Write number pair facts

Use your knowledge of place value to complete this diagram.

- Write some pairs to 100, 10 and 1. One is done for you.
- Use your knowledge of number bonds to 10 to help you.

Key words
- number pairs
- known facts
- derive

Use both decimals and fractions if you can.

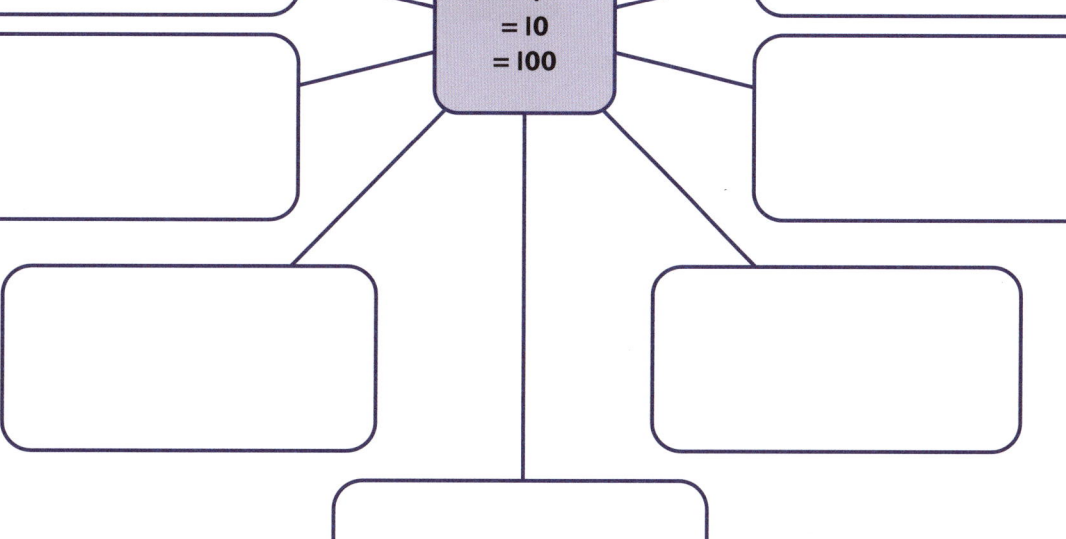

76 + 24 = 100
7.6 + 2.4 = 10
0.76 + 0.24 = 1

= 1
= 10
= 100

Stretch zone

Use one of your pairs to write pairs to 1000, 10 000 and 100 000.

19

1. Number and place value

■ For more practice, go to Practice Book 6, page 24.

1 Number and place value

Connect

Chessboard and rice problem

In 1256, the Islamic scholar Ibn Khallikan wrote the following maths problem. A king wanted to reward a wise man for inventing the game of chess. He asked the man what reward he would like. The wise man replied:

I only want one small gift. Tomorrow, place one grain of rice on the first square of your chessboard. I will take this home for my family. On the second day place two grains on the next square for me. On the third day double the number of grains again, placing four grains for me to take home. Each day double the number of grains you give me until you have placed rice on every square of the chessboard. That will be sufficient reward for me.

1 How many squares do you think it will take to reach one million grains of rice on the chessboard?

   a   Estimate the answer. [ ] squares

   b   Now calculate the answer. [ ] squares

2 How far can you get calculating mentally? [ ] squares

   [ ] grains of rice

3 Now use a calculator to do the calculations.

   When does your calculator run out of digits? [ ] squares

   [ ] grains of rice

Stretch zone

Calculate the answer to **question 1** using rounding. When your answer is above 10 round to the nearest 10; when it is above 100 round to the nearest 100; when it is above 1000 round to the nearest 1000 and so on. Does this make the problem easier to solve? Explain your answer.

1 Number and place value

1 Write the number five million, thirty-six thousand and fourteen in numerals.

2 What is the value of 3 in the number 403 526?

3 Write 6 102 120 in words. _____

_____

4 Fill in the missing numbers in this number sentence.

356 841 = 300 000 + [   ] + [   ] + 800 + 40 + [   ]

5 What number is 200 000 more than 3 465 215?

6 What is 526 × 1000?

7 The population of a country is 8 256 853.
Round the population to:

a the nearest 10

b the nearest 100

c the nearest 1000.

8 Use the < and > symbols to make these statements correct.

a ⁻32 [ ] ⁻15

b ⁻18 [ ] ⁻16

c ⁻18 [ ] ⁻20

9 The temperature in my apartment is 22 °C. Outside the temperature is ⁻8 °C.

How much colder is it outside? [   ] °C

In this unit you will:

- perform mental calculations, including with mixed operations and large numbers
- use estimation to check answers to calculations
- solve addition, subtraction, multiplication and division problems using written methods
- interpret remainders to division problems as whole number remainders or fractions
- identify common factors, common multiples and prime numbers
- use your knowledge of the order of operations to carry out calculations involving the four operations.

?

Which are the most efficient strategies for carrying out calculations?

I know that 300×30 is 9000, so the answer will be a little less than 9000.

Engage

How can you calculate 286×29?

There are different ways to work it out.

Which way do you think is easiest?

Which way do you think is quickest?

2A Mental strategies for addition and subtraction

Discover

Two-digit number problems

1 This table gives the numbers of students in each class in a school.

Class	Number of students
Kindergarten	42
Class 1	28
Class 2	35
Class 3	33
Class 4	35
Class 5	33
Class 6	27

Key words
- addition
- subtraction
- mental strategies
- bonds to 10

Try to spot bonds to 10. I know that $33 + 27 = 60$ because $3 + 7 = 10$

Finding doubles can help too.

Use two different strategies to work out the total number of students in the school.

Total number of students: ☐   Check: ☐

2 This table shows how many people got on and off a bus at each stop.

Stop	Number that got on the bus	Number that got off the bus
Bus station	38	0
Cinema	9	5
School	15	3
Ice rink	11	12
Shopping mall	26	14
Riverside	7	9
Stadium	3	24

Use your second strategy to check your answer.

Work with a partner.

- One student reads out loud the information from the table.
- The other student writes the number of people on the bus when it leaves the stadium. ☐

Stretch zone

Explain your strategies to each other. Which was the most efficient strategy?

■ For more practice, go to Practice Book 6, page 26.

2A Mental strategies for addition and subtraction

Explore

Use mental strategies to add and subtract

| 1 | 2 | 3 | 4 | 5 | 6 | 7 |

Key words
- sum
- difference
- addition
- subtraction

Use all of the digits 1–7 once in each of the following calculations.

1 Write an addition with two numbers.

_____

2 Write an addition with three numbers.

_____

3 Write a subtraction with two numbers.

_____

4 Write calculations to find:

a the largest sum with two numbers

_____

b the largest sum with three numbers

_____

c the smallest sum with two numbers

_____

d the smallest sum with three numbers

_____

e the largest difference between two numbers

_____

f the smallest difference between two numbers.

_____

I wrote $1234 + 567 = 1801$

I wrote
$123 + 45 + 67 = 235$

I wrote $3124 - 567 = 2557$

Stretch zone

Try to find a quick way to add together all the numbers from 1 to 100.

24

2B Mental strategies for multiplication and division

Discover 1

Divisibility rules and mental multiplication

Key words
- multiplication
- division
- divisibility rules
- mental strategy

1 Work in a group. Find the divisibility rules for each of the multiplication tables below. Write the rules.

Multiplication table	Rule
× 2	A number is divisible by 2 if
× 3	A number is divisible by 3 if
× 4	A number is divisible by 4 if
× 5	A number is divisible by 5 if
× 6	A number is divisible by 6 if
× 8	A number is divisible by 8 if
× 9	A number is divisible by 9 if
× 10	A number is divisible by 10 if

2 Complete these calculations.

a $15 \times 9 =$ ☐

b $16 \times 9 =$ ☐

c $17 \times 9 =$ ☐

d $18 \times 9 =$ ☐

e $19 \times 9 =$ ☐

f $20 \times 9 =$ ☐

g $21 \times 9 =$ ☐

h $15 \times 11 =$ ☐

i $16 \times 11 =$ ☐

j $17 \times 11 =$ ☐

k $18 \times 11 =$ ☐

l $19 \times 11 =$ ☐

m $20 \times 11 =$ ☐

n $21 \times 11 =$ ☐

Talk to a partner about the strategies you used to work out the answers.

Stretch zone

Work out the divisibility rule for 7. Explain the rule to a partner.

■ For more practice, go to Practice Book 6, page 28.

2B Mental strategies for multiplication and division

Discover 2

Use known facts to multiply

Key words
- multiplication
- mental strategy

1 Complete this multiplication table.

×	0.25	0.5	5	10	50	70	100
3							
6							
9							
10							
30							
60							
70							

Talk to a partner about the strategies you used.

2 Create a multiplication table for your partner to complete.

×							

Look at the patterns in the table in **question 1**. Use these to help you choose good numbers to write in the first row and the first column in this table.

Stretch zone

Write the 17 times table. What strategies did you use to work it out?

■ For more practice, go to Practice Book 6, page 29.

2B Mental strategies for multiplication and division

Explore 1

Multiplication rules

Key words
- multiples of 10
- mental strategy

I Complete the multiplication table. It includes multiples of 10, near multiples of 10 and numbers with one decimal place.

- First do the calculations mentally.
- Then check your results using a different method.

×	10	25	30	50	60	90
20						
30						
40						
70						
19						
21						
39						
51						
0.2						
0.4						
0.8						
0.5						
0.9						

2 What mental strategies do you use? Complete these sentences.

a To multiply by multiples of 10, I _____

_____

b To multiply by near multiples of 10, I _____

_____

c To multiply by numbers with one decimal place, I

_____

_____

Stretch zone

Write a general rule for multiplying or dividing a number by any multiple of 10.

2 Addition, subtraction, multiplication and division

■ For more practice, go to Practice Book 6, page 30.

2B Mental strategies for multiplication and division

Explore 2

Use known facts to multiply and divide

Think back

We can use one number fact to derive lots of other facts.

I know that $7 \times 6 = 42$, so I can work out $70 \times 6 = 420$ because 70 is ten times bigger than 7.

$4.2 \div 6 = 0.7$ because 4.2 is ten times smaller than 42.

7×12 is 84 because 12 is double 6.

Complete this diagram with new facts that you can derive from $8 \times 7 = 56$. Two are done for you.

You can use multiples of 10, decimals, doubles and halves and near multiples.

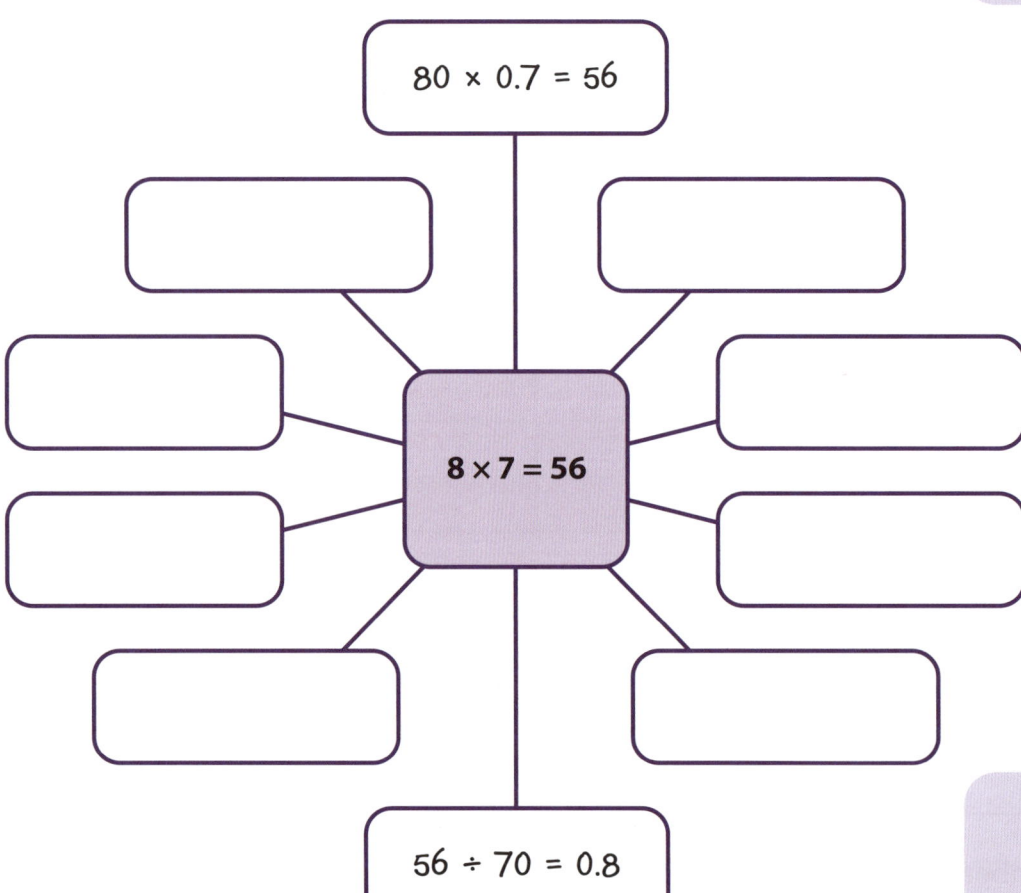

$80 \times 0.7 = 56$

$8 \times 7 = 56$

$56 \div 70 = 0.8$

Use a mixture of multiplication and division.

Stretch zone

Write ten new facts you can derive from $19 \times 20 = 380$. Include five multiplication facts and five division facts.

■ For more practice, go to Practice Book 6, page 31.

2C Adding and subtracting near multiples

Discover

Add or subtract multiples and adjust

Complete the calculations in this table. Write the strategy that you used.

Key words
- addition
- subtraction
- mental strategy

	Calculation	Strategy and answer
1	54 + 19	
2	5.4 + 2.9	
3	107 – 98	
4	1107 – 198	
5	17.5 – 3.1	
6	17.5 – 3.6	
7	6743 – 2997	
8	6743 – 3998	
9	99 + 25	
10	999 + 25	
11	852 – 303	

I worked out 36 + 9 = 45. First I worked out 36 + 10 = 46 and then I subtracted 1.

I worked out 5625 – 999 = 4626. First I subtracted 1000 and then I added 1.

Stretch zone

Write an addition or subtraction calculation with a near multiple that it is easy to solve mentally. Write another calculation that is difficult to solve mentally.

■ For more practice, go to Practice Book 6, page 32.

2C Adding and subtracting near multiples

Explore

Money calculations with near multiples

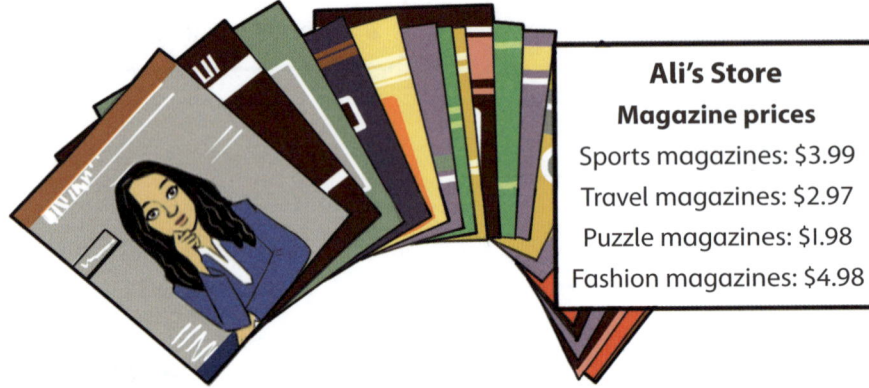

Ali's Store
Magazine prices

Sports magazines: $3.99

Travel magazines: $2.97

Puzzle magazines: $1.98

Fashion magazines: $4.98

Key words
- sum
- difference
- addition
- subtraction

I have $5. I buy a puzzle magazine. How much money do I have left?

I Look at the prices of the magazines.

Write six word problems about the magazines. Write three addition problems and three subtraction problems.

a _____

d _____

b _____

e _____

c _____

f _____

 **2** Swap books with a partner and solve their problems.

Stretch zone

Compare the strategies you used. What different strategies could you have used?

■ For more practice, go to Practice Book 6, page 33.

2D Estimating first in calculations

Discover

Key words
- estimate
- sum
- smallest
- largest
- place value

Estimate to find the answers

Use all these digits to make additions with two 3-digit numbers.

| 4 | 5 | 6 | 7 | 8 | 9 |

- Use each digit only once in each calculation.

1 Write an addition with:

  a the smallest possible total

  b the largest possible total.

2 Write additions with answers that are as close as possible to the numbers in the table.

900	1200
1300	1400
1500	1600
1700	1800

Estimate the answer first by rounding to see if your answer is sensible.

I made 546 + 879. I estimated the answer first: 550 + 900 = 1450, then I worked out the answer: 1425

I tried to get close to 900: 576 + 489 = 1065. Can you make a sum that is closer to 900?

Stretch zone

Now the rules have changed: you can use the digits more than once in a calculation and you do not have to use all the digits. Write additions with answers that are closer to the numbers in the table.

■ For more practice, go to Practice Book 6, page 34.

Explore

Check answers

Check these calculations.

- If they are correct, tick them.
- If there is an error, explain the error and correct it.

Key words
- written method
- column method
- recombine

Use estimation and facts that you know to check each calculation.

1 $\begin{array}{r} 983 \\ -\ 664 \\ \hline 319 \end{array}$	**6** $\begin{array}{r} 27.5 \\ +\ 42.6 \\ \hline 69.11 \end{array}$
2 $\begin{array}{r} 456 \\ +\ 845 \\ \hline 1291 \end{array}$	**7** $\begin{array}{r} 38.9 \\ +\ 46.5 \\ \hline 85.4 \end{array}$
3 $\begin{array}{r} 876 \\ -\ 459 \\ \hline 417 \end{array}$	**8** $\begin{array}{r} 76.5 \\ -\ 32.8 \\ \hline 43.7 \end{array}$
4 $\begin{array}{r} 84.7 \\ -\ 36.9 \\ \hline 52.2 \end{array}$	**9** $\begin{array}{r} 576 \\ +\ 345 \\ \hline 921 \end{array}$
5 $\begin{array}{r} 346 \\ +\ 504 \\ \hline 840 \end{array}$	**10** $\begin{array}{r} 1000 \\ -\ \ \ \ 2 \\ \hline 9998 \end{array}$

Stretch zone

Write an addition calculation and a subtraction calculation with a deliberate mistake in each. Can your partner spot the mistakes?

32

■ For more practice, go to Practice Book 6, page 35.

Discover

Key words in problems

Think back

Which words tell you the operation to use? Look out for the key words.

Key words
- total
- difference
- how much longer/bigger/smaller?
- how much is left?

Read these problems. Underline the key information in each problem first, then solve the problem.

1 I post two parcels. One parcel has a mass of 3.56 kg.

The other parcel has a mass of 4.82 kg.

a What is the total mass of the parcels?

b What is the difference between the masses of the two parcels?

Which operation do you need to use for each part of this problem? How do you know?

2 The area of our classroom wall is 15.73 m^2.

The area of the whiteboard is 2.29 m^2.

The area of the noticeboard is 3.58 m^2.

How much space is left on the wall?

This is a two-part problem, involving both addition and subtraction. Which do you need to do first?

Stretch zone

Make up a word problem for a partner to solve. Use key words in your problem that tell your partner which operation to use.

2 Addition, subtraction, multiplication and division

33

2E Which operation?

Explore

Solve word problems

Solve these problems. First identify which operation to use, then solve the problem.

1 I have a 50 gigabyte (GB) data allowance per month on my phone contract.

I use 18.85 GB to download music and 23.65 GB to download movies.

How much of my allowance do I have left?

Key words
- total
- difference
- how much longer/bigger/smaller?
- how much is left?

Show your workings in your notebook.

2 In a 4 × 100 m relay race the four runners' times are 16.46 s, 17.15 s, 15.52 s and 14.99 s.

What is the total time of the four runners?

Remember to include the units in your answers.

3 Hassan and Rosa buy some new games for their games consoles.

a Hassan buys Parkour Star and Underwater Adventure. How much does he spend in total?

$ _____

Wild Animal Rescue

$18.95

b Rosa buys Wild Animal Rescue and Parkour Star. She pays with a $50 note. How much change does she receive?

$ _____

PARKOUR STAR

$22.99

UNDERWATER ADVENTURE

$24.55

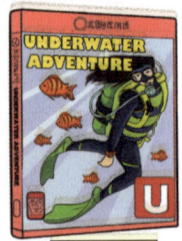

Stretch zone

Write two more questions using the prices of the games in **question 3**. Swap your questions with a partner.

■ For more practice, go to Practice Book 6, page 37.

2F Multiplying 3- and 4-digit numbers

Discover

Multiply large numbers

Think back

We can use different strategies to multiply larger numbers. For example, we can:

- partition the number and multiply the individual parts
- use a grid method
- use a column method.

Key words
- partitioning
- grid method
- column method

Check your answers are sensible by estimating.

 1 Use partitioning to solve these multiplications.

a $346 \times 7 = ($ ⬚ $\times 7) + (40 \times$ ⬚ $) + ($ ⬚ $\times 7) =$ ⬚

b $\$4.92 \times 3 = (4 \times 3) + (0.9 \times$ ⬚ $) + ($ ⬚ $\times 3) =$ ⬚

c $685 \times 6 = ($ ⬚ $\times 6) + (80 \times$ ⬚ $) + ($ ⬚ $\times 6) =$ ⬚

d $\$4.56 \times 4 = ($ ⬚ $\times 4) + (0.5 \times$ ⬚ $) + ($ ⬚ $\times 4) =$ ⬚

e $532 \times 8 =$ ⬚

f $\$8.26 \times 5 =$ ⬚

 2 Max does not understand this grid multiplication. Complete the sentences below to explain it to him.

×	40	7	
300	12 000	2100	14 100
60	2400	420	2820
5	200	35	235
			17 155

This multiplication shows $365 \times$ ⬚ .

12 000 is the answer to $300 \times$ ⬚ .

The first column contains 300, 60 and 5 because _____.

2820 is in the same row as 60 because _____.

I calculate the answer 17 155 by _____.

Discover (continued)

3 Complete the grid below to calculate 523×47.

My estimate is _____ .

×		**7**	
500	20 000		
		140	940
3		21	

I worked out 500 × 50 as my estimate.

4 Use the grid below to calculate 426×82.

My estimate is _____ .

×			

Partition 426 in the first column and 82 in the top row.

5 Eric does not understand this column multiplication. Complete the sentences below to explain it to him.

		3	5	2
	×		6	3
	1	0	5	6
2	1	1	2	0
2	2	1	7	6

1056 is the answer to _____

21 120 is the answer to _____

I get 22 176 by _____

_____

Stretch zone

Write a set of instructions to explain how to calculate 415×27 using the column method.

■ For more practice, go to Practice Book 6, page 38.

Explore

Product investigation

Think back

The product is the answer when we multiply two or more numbers.

Key words
- product
- column method

Use each of these digits only once to make a multiplication calculation.

| 4 | 5 | 6 | 7 | 8 |

I Investigate the largest product you can make using these digits.

- Use the column method to do the calculations.

I will try 45 × 678 first and then 4 × 5678.

2 What calculation will make the largest product using these digits?

| 3 | 4 | 5 | 6 | 7 | 8 | 9 |

I know I need to use the largest digits in the columns with the largest place value.

Stretch zone

Explain to a partner why you are sure you have found the largest product in **question 1**. Work out the answer to your calculation in **question 2**.

■ For more practice, go to Practice Book 6, page 39.

2 Addition, subtraction, multiplication and division

2G Long division

Discover

Explain long division

Think back

The dividend is the number you divide. The divisor is the number you divide by. The quotient is the answer.

dividend   divisor   quotient

$$845 \div 13 = 65$$

1   Harriet does not understand how to calculate $858 \div 13$.

Complete the sentences below to explain the method to her.

```
          6  6
1  3 ) 8  5  8
       7  8  0      60 × 13 = 780
          7  8       6 × 13 = 78
```

I tried 60×13 first because _____

_____

I know that $6 \times 13 = 78$ because _____

_____

The answer is 66 because _____

_____

You can check the answer by _____

2   Fill in the blanks to calculate $756 \div 14$.

```
            □ □
□ □ ) 7  5  6
      7  0  0      □0 × □□ = 700
         5  6      □ × □□ = 56
```

Stretch zone

Write a long division calculation that has a quotient of 63. Show each line of your workings.

■ For more practice, go to Practice Book 6, page 40.

2G Long division

Explore

Long division problems

Solve these problems. Use a long division method to show that you are correct.

1 The answer to a division question is 131 apples.

- Use the digits 1, 2, 3, 4, 4 and 4 to find the 4-digit dividend and the 2-digit divisor.

Use what you know about inverse operations to help you find the answers.

2 The answer to a division question is 15 tins.

- Use the digits 0, 1, 2, 7 and 8 to find the 3-digit dividend and the 2-digit divisor.

Show all your workings.

3 The answer to a division question is 52 stickers.

- Use the digits 1, 2, 2, 3, 5 and 6 to find the 4-digit dividend and the 2-digit divisor.

Stretch zone

Write a long division calculation using the digits 5, 6, 7 and 8 for the dividend and divisor. You can use the digits more than once. Give the answer to a partner and ask them to work out the question. There should be no remainder.

■ For more practice, go to Practice Book 6, page 41.

2 Addition, subtraction, multiplication and division

2H Short division

Discover

Explain short division

Think back

You can use a multiplication to check the answer to a division problem.

Key words
- written method
- dividend
- divisor
- quotient

1 Complete these steps that explain how to calculate 2193 ÷ 17 using short division.

$$\begin{array}{r} 0\ 1\ 2\ 9 \\ 17\overline{)2\ ^2 1\ ^4 9\ ^{15}3} \end{array}$$

a First I estimated the answer: ⬚

b I wrote '0' above the '2' because 17 does not go into ⬚ thousands.

c The next calculation is 21 ÷ 17 because I exchanged the 2 thousands for ⬚ hundreds.

d I wrote '1' above '21' because 17 goes into ⬚ hundreds 1 time with ⬚ hundreds left over.

e The next calculation is 49 ÷ 17 because there were 4 hundreds left over, which I exchanged for ⬚ tens.

f I wrote '2' above '49' because 17 goes into ⬚ tens 2 times with ⬚ tens left over.

g The final calculation is 153 ÷ 17 because there were ⬚ tens left over, which I exchanged for ⬚ ones.

h I wrote '9' above '153' because 17 goes into ⬚ ones ⬚ times.

i The final answer is ⬚.

j I checked my answer by doing a _____ calculation: 129 ⬚ 17 = ⬚

> This time there is a remainder.

2 Use short division to calculate 9037 ÷ 14.

Stretch zone

Write a short division calculation with a quotient of 152.

■ For more practice, go to Practice Book 6, page 42.

2H Short division

Explore

Short division problems

1 The answer to a division question is 28 stamps.

- Use only the digits 0, 1, 2, 4 and 5 to find the 3-digit dividend and the 2-digit divisor.
- Use a short division method to show that you are correct.

Remember to use what you know about inverse operations to help you find the answers.

2 Write two different possible short division calculations for each question.

a The answer to a division question is 35 apples. The divisor is a 2-digit number.

b The quotient is 152. The dividend has 4 digits.

Stretch zone

Write a question like **question 1**. It should not have a remainder. Give your question to a partner to solve. Use a multiplication to check their answer.

■ For more practice, go to Practice Book 6, page 43.

21 Division with remainders

Discover

Remainders as fractions and decimals

1 Write three different division calculations with an answer that includes a remainder of 3.

a

b

c

2 Write three different division calculations with a mixed number answer that includes $\frac{3}{4}$.

a

b

c

3 Write three different division calculations with a decimal number answer that includes 0.25

a

b

c

I wrote $45 \div 7 = 6$ r 3. I know there will be remainder 3 because $7 \times 6 = 42$.

I wrote $43 \div 4 = 10\frac{3}{4}$ because $4 \times 10 = 40$ and there are 3 left over. We are dividing by 4 so that leaves $\frac{3}{4}$.

I wrote $49 \div 4 = 12.25$ because $4 \times 12 = 48$ and there is 1 left over. We are dividing by 4 so that leaves $\frac{1}{4}$, which I wrote as a decimal.

Discover (continued)

4 Complete the following sentences to explain how to carry out this calculation:

$$5 \overline{)7\ ^28\ .\ ^30} = 1\ 5\ .\ 6$$

This calculation shows how to work out 78 ÷ ☐

I wrote '1' above the '70' because _____

_____

The next calculation is 28 ÷ 5 because _____

_____

The final answer is 15.6 because _____

_____

You divide with decimals in exactly the same way as when you divide with whole numbers.

5 Write two calculations to divide a 3-digit number with one decimal place by a single-digit number.

Work out your calculations.

● **Stretch zone**

Check your answers to your division questions in **question 5** by writing the multiplication calculation to match each division.

2 Addition, subtraction, multiplication and division

■ For more practice, go to Practice Book 6, page 44.

21 Division with remainders

Explore

Transport and shopping problems

3562 children from local schools are going on a school trip.

- A minibus holds 14 children.
- A coach holds 38 children.
- A double-decker coach holds 65 children.

Key words
- dividend
- divisor
- quotient
- remainder

1 If all the children travel by minibus, how many minibuses do they need?

Are all the minibuses full? _____

How many children are in each minibus?

2 If all the children travel by coach, how many coaches do they need?

Are all the coaches full? _____

How many children are in each coach?

Show all your workings.

3 If all the children travel by double-decker coach, how many double-decker coaches do they need?

Are all the double-decker coaches full? _____

How many children are in each coach?

2I Division with remainders

Explore (continued)

4 Imran wants to get a good deal at the shop.

- Work out the price of each item in each pack or box.
- Circle the better deal for each item.
- Show all your workings in your notebook.

5 Use the price of an individual item from the better deal to work out the cost of:

a 24 ice lollies $ _____

b 27 cakes $ _____

c 35 bottles of juice. $ _____

a

Washing powder:
$18.92 for a 2 kg box
$50.54 for a 7 kg box

b

Juice:
$14.35 for a 5-bottle pack
$19.39 for a 7-bottle pack

c

Ice lollies:
$6.80 for a box of 20
$4.44 for a box of 12

d

Cakes:
$18.06 for a box of 14
$15.72 for a box of 12

e

Iced tea:
$42.96 for 24
$21.60 for 12

Stretch zone

Look at **page 44**. How can you organise the travel to use the smallest possible number of vehicles?

■ For more practice, go to Practice Book 6, page 45.

2J Factors, multiples and primes

Discover

Find factors and prime numbers

Key words
- prime number
- composite number

Think back

A factor of a number is a number that divides exactly into that number.

This array shows that we can write 24 as 3×8.

8 and 3 are factors of 24. Both numbers divide exactly into 24.

1 How many ways can you arrange 24 cubes?

● Draw all the different ways.

● Then complete this sentence.

The factors of 24 are ⬚

2 Repeat this for 18, 36, 49 and 64 cubes. Draw the arrays in your notebook.

● Then complete these sentences.

a The factors of 18 are ⬚

b The factors of 36 are ⬚

c The factors of 49 are ⬚

d The factors of 64 are ⬚

Discover (continued)

Think back

A prime number is a number that has only two factors: 1 and itself.

3 Colour all the prime numbers between 2 and 100 on this 100-square.

1	2	3	4	5	6	7	8	9	10
11	12	13	14	15	16	17	18	19	20
21	22	23	24	25	26	27	28	29	30
31	32	33	34	35	36	37	38	39	40
41	42	43	44	45	46	47	48	49	50
51	52	53	54	55	56	57	58	59	60
61	62	63	64	65	66	67	68	69	70
71	72	73	74	75	76	77	78	79	80
81	82	83	84	85	86	87	88	89	90
91	92	93	94	95	96	97	98	99	100

How do you know if a number is prime?

4 Enzo says that 201 is a prime number. Is he correct? Explain how you know.

_____

_____

Stretch zone

Predict how many prime numbers there are between 100 and 120. Explain your prediction and then check if you are correct.

■ For more practice, go to Practice Book 6, page 46.

2J Factors, multiples and primes

Find prime factors and common multiples

Think back

A composite number is a number that has more than two factors.

A prime factor is a factor that is also a prime number. You can divide all composite numbers into prime factors.

You can use a factor tree to find the prime factors of any number.

Worked example

80 — 80 has factors 2 and 40

2 is a prime factor of 80 — 2, 40 — 40 has factors 4 and 10

4 is not a prime number — 4, 10 — 10 is not a prime number

$4 = 2 \times 2$ — 2, 2, 2, 5 — $10 = 2 \times 5$

2 is a prime factor — 2 and 5 are prime factors

The numbers in green circles in the factor tree are the prime factors of 80.

$80 = 2 \times 2 \times 2 \times 2 \times 5$ 2, 2, 2, 2 and 5 are the prime factors of 80.

1 Find the prime factors of these numbers.

 150   36   75

Draw a factor tree for each number.

Explore (continued)

We know that 1, 2, 3, 4, 6 and 12 are factors of 12. They divide exactly into 12.

We can also say that 12 is a multiple of 1, 2, 3, 4, 6 and 12 because it is in the multiplication tables for all these numbers.

If a number is in more than one multiplication table, we say it is a common multiple of those numbers. 12 is a common multiple of 1, 2, 3, 4, 6 and 12.

2 Complete this Venn diagram to show numbers less than 50 that are multiples and common multiples of 4 and 6.

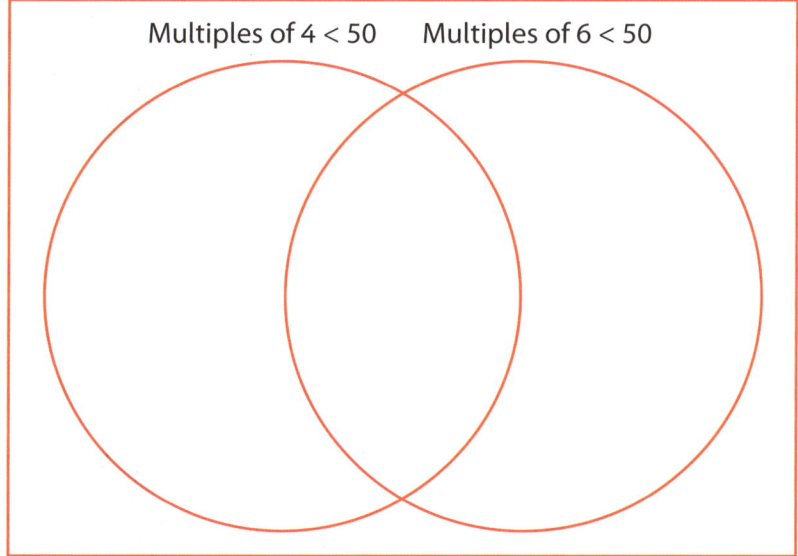

Multiples of 4 < 50   Multiples of 6 < 50

The numbers in both multiplication tables are the common multiples of 4 and 6. These go in the intersection.

3 Write the common multiples less than 50 of these numbers.

3 and 7

2 and 10

4 and 12

6 and 9

What is the lowest common multiple of each pair of numbers?

Stretch zone

Find the common multiples of 2, 3 and 5 up to 50. Draw a Venn diagram with three circles to show the common multiples.

2K Order of operations

Discover

Key words
- brackets
- order of operations

Order of operations

I Aisha calculates $5 \times 3 + 7$. She says that $5 \times 3 + 7 = 50$

Explain how she got the answer 50. _____

_____

2 Simran calculates $5 \times 3 + 7$. She says that $5 \times 3 + 7 = 22$

Explain how she got the answer 22. _____

_____

3 What answer does your calculator show for the calculation $5 \times 3 + 7$?

Who do you think is correct, Aisha or Simran?

> **Worked example**
>
> We can write $(5 \times 3) + 7 = 22$ but
>
> $5 \times (3 + 7) = 50$

The brackets tell us which part to do first.

4 Mark these calculations correct ✓ or incorrect ✗.

- If the calculation is incorrect, rewrite the calculation in the box, with the brackets in the correct place.

  a $6 \times (5 - 3) = 27$

  b $2 + (9 \times 5) = 55$

  c $(25 \div 5) - 6 = ^-1$

  d $15 - (12 \div 4) = 12$

  e $(4 \times 3) + (7 \times 2) = 80$

Stretch zone

Write a calculation including brackets and using all four operations with the answer 2.

50

2K Order of operations

Explore

BIDMAS

Key words
- brackets
- order of operations
- BIDMAS

This is the order for carrying out operations in a calculation.

B	(brackets)
I	indices^2
D	÷ division
M	multiplication ×
A	+ addition
S	subtraction −

Use the order of operations to make all the numbers from 1 to 20 using only the digits 1, 2, 3 and 4.

1	11
2	12
3	13
4	14
5	15
6	16
7	17
8	18
9	19
10	20

I can make
$11 = 2 × 3 + (1 + 4)$

I can make
$20 = 1 × 4 × (2 + 3)$

Stretch zone

Can you make all the numbers from 21 to 40, using only the digits 1, 2, 3 and 4 and the BIDMAS order of operations?

■ For more practice, go to Practice Book 6, page 49.

2 Addition, subtraction, multiplication and division

2L Using the arithmetical laws

Discover

Key words
- commutative law
- associative law
- distributive law

The arithmetical laws

1 Work in pairs. Research the meanings of the following mathematical terms. Write an example of each one.

The associative law

The commutative law

The distributive law

> I used the internet to find out about these laws. You may have a mathematics dictionary in your classroom that you can use.

2 Is each statement true or false?

- Circle the correct answer.
- Write one example for each statement to support your answer.

a I can add numbers in any order and I get the same answer.

True / False

b I can multiply numbers in any order and I get the same answer.

True / False

c $a(b + c)$ is the same as $ab + ac$

True / False

d I can subtract numbers in any order and I get the same answer.

True / False

e I can divide numbers in any order and I get the same answer.

True / False

f $\frac{a+b}{c}$ is the same as $\frac{a}{c} + \frac{b}{c}$

True / False

Stretch zone

Make a poster for your word wall to explain these three arithmetical laws.

■ For more practice, go to Practice Book 6, page 50.

2L Using the arithmetical laws

Explore

Apply the arithmetical laws

Key words
- commutative law
- associative law
- distributive law

I Use the commutative law to make each multiplication easier to work out. Then calculate the answer.

Worked example

Here is an example of the commutative law:

$12 \times 16 \times 5 \quad = \quad 12 \times 5 \times 16 \quad = \quad 60 \times 16 = 960$

a $20 \times 18 \times 5 =$

b $15 \times 13 \times 10 =$

c $18 \times 25 \times 4 =$

d $5 \times 15 \times 2 =$

e $4 \times 26 \times 5 =$

f $6 \times 25 \times 7 =$

2 Use the distributive law to make each multiplication easier to work out. Then calculate the answer.

Worked example

Here is an example of the distributive law:

$46 \times 8 \quad = \quad (40 + 6) \times 8$

$= (40 \times 8) + (6 \times 8) = 320 + 48 = 368$

Write your calculations clearly. Look at the worked examples to help you.

a $27 \times 6 =$

b $38 \times 5 =$

c $58 \times 7 =$

d $62 \times 9 =$

e $55 \times 8 =$

f $73 \times 9 =$

2L Using the arithmetical laws

Explore (continued)

3 Use the associative law to make each multiplication easier to work out. Then calculate the answer.

> **Worked example**
>
> Here is an example of the associative law:
>
> 14×9
>
> $= (2 \times 7) \times 9$
>
> $= 2 \times (7 \times 9)$
>
> $= 2 \times 63 = 126$

a 16×8	**d** 18×9
b 16×9	**e** 24×8
c 18×7	**f** 35×6

Write your calculations clearly. Use a different line for each step of the calculation. Look at the worked example to help you.

Stretch zone

Discuss with a partner which law is used in each calculation below. Do you agree that using the law makes the calculation easier? Explain your answers.

34×8

$= (30 \times 8) + (4 \times 8)$

$= 240 + 32 = 272$

35×8

$= (5 \times 7) \times 8$

$= 5 \times (7 \times 8)$

$= 5 \times 56 = 280$

$30 \times 12 \times 5$

$= 12 \times 5 \times 30$

$= 60 \times 30 = 1800$

■ For more practice, go to Practice Book 6, page 51.

2 Addition, subtraction, multiplication and division

Connect

Closest to...

1 Play this game in a group.

- Pick one card at a time from a set of digit cards 1–9.
- Write each digit, as you pick it, in the addition grid.
- The aim is to get the closest possible answer to 100.
- Add your three numbers.
- Who was closest to 100?

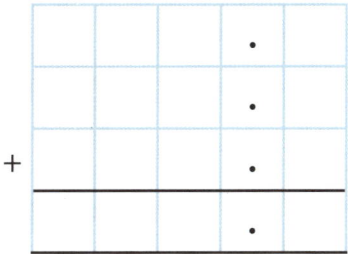

2 Play again, using this subtraction grid.

- Pick six digits.
- The aim is to get the closest possible answer to 10.

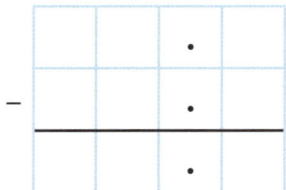

3 Play again, using this multiplication grid.

- Pick four digits.
- The aim is to get the closest possible answer to 1000.

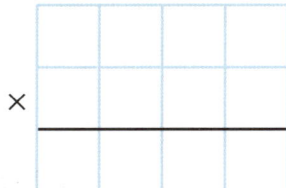

4 Play again, using this division grid.

- Pick five digits.
- The aim is to get the closest possible answer to 10.

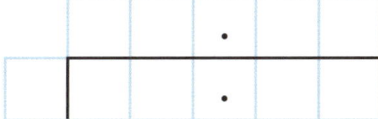

> We can use mental or written strategies to solve calculations. The best strategy to use depends on the numbers. I have learned to find the most efficient strategy.

My addition is:
$$\begin{aligned} 18.7 \\ + 32.9 \\ \underline{45.6} \\ \underline{97.2} \end{aligned}$$

My subtraction is:
$25.3 - 14.9 = 10.4$

My multiplication is:
$261 \times 4 = 1044$

My division is
$68.25 \div 7 = 9.75$

2 Addition, subtraction, multiplication and division

1 8545 + 124 =

2 ☐ + 18 = 359

3 9 × 51 =

4 6.87 + 3.121 =

5 180 ÷ 6 =

6 191 ÷ 7 =

7 60 ÷ (30 − 5) =

How will you write your remainders? As a remainder, a fraction or a decimal?

8 816 × 23

10 3145 ÷ 37

9 783 ÷ 29

11 A machine pours 500 millilitres of water every 30 seconds. How much water does the machine pour in 10 minutes?

Hint: Remember that there are 1000 millilitres in 1 litre.

3 Fractions, decimals and percentages

In this unit you will:

- use common factors to simplify fractions and use common multiples to write fractions with the same denominator
- compare and order fractions, including fractions greater than 1
- add, subtract, multiply and divide fractions and decimals
- convert fractions to decimals and decimals to fractions
- understand place value in numbers with up to 3 decimal places
- solve problems involving fractions, decimals and percentages.

? How do I use fractions, decimals and percentages to solve mathematical problems in everyday contexts?

Engage

What is the same and what is different about fractions and percentages?

Which is better: 20% off or a reduction of $\frac{1}{3}$?

Why do we need fractions and percentages?

Where do you see fractions and percentages in everyday life?

Discover

Key words
- simplest form
- equivalent fraction

Different equivalents

The fraction $\frac{3}{5}$ is equivalent to $\frac{6}{10}$.

$\frac{3}{5}$ is the simplest form of this fraction.

Complete the table.

Fraction in its simplest form	Fraction in words	Bar model	Equivalent fraction	A different equivalent fraction
$\frac{3}{5}$	three fifths		$\frac{6}{10}$	$\frac{9}{15}$
				$\frac{50}{100}$
	four fifths			
$\frac{1}{4}$				
$\frac{3}{4}$			$\frac{9}{12}$	
				$\frac{4}{12}$

Stretch zone

Choose your own fractions for the last two rows. Choose one fraction that is easy to simplify and one fraction that is difficult to simplify.

■ For more practice, go to Practice Book 6, page 53.

3A Equivalent fractions

Explore

Use equivalent fractions to order a set

Key words
- simplest form
- equivalent fraction

Think back

To order a set of fractions, use equivalent fractions.

For example, to order $\frac{1}{2}, \frac{2}{3}, \frac{3}{8}, \frac{5}{6}, \frac{1}{4}, \frac{7}{8}, \frac{3}{4}$

we know that $\frac{3}{4} = \frac{6}{8}$ so $\frac{3}{4} < \frac{7}{8}$

The correct order, starting with the smallest, is:

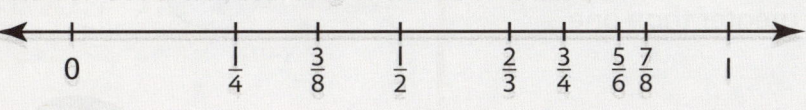

1. Find pairs of equivalent fractions in this set. Use a different colour to circle each pair.

$$\frac{1}{4} \quad \frac{3}{12} \quad \frac{4}{10} \quad \frac{9}{12} \quad \frac{5}{6} \quad \frac{2}{5} \quad \frac{1}{2} \quad \frac{3}{4} \quad \frac{10}{12} \quad \frac{6}{12}$$

2. Write each pair in the correct position on the number line.

   - Write the fraction in its simplest form above the line.
   - Write the equivalent fraction below the number line.

3. Order these fractions on the number line.

   - Write an equivalent fraction for each fraction below the number line.

   $$\frac{3}{4} \quad \frac{10}{12} \quad \frac{1}{3} \quad \frac{1}{2} \quad \frac{4}{5} \quad \frac{2}{3}$$

Start with the ones you definitely know. Then work out where the others must go.

Stretch zone

Order this set of fractions.

$$\frac{4}{5} \quad \frac{3}{10} \quad \frac{1}{2} \quad \frac{9}{10} \quad \frac{2}{5} \quad \frac{4}{15} \quad \frac{2}{3}$$

Start with the smallest. Write an equivalent fraction for each fraction. Explain how you know that the fractions are in the correct order.

3 Fractions, decimals and percentages

■ For more practice, go to Practice Book 6, page 54.

3B Mixed numbers and improper fractions

Discover

Equivalent improper fractions and mixed numbers

Think back

An improper fraction has a numerator that is greater than its denominator. This means that an improper fraction is greater than 1.

$\frac{5}{4}$ is an improper fraction.

Four quarters make a whole, so $\frac{5}{4}$ is greater than one. $\frac{5}{4}$ is the same as $1\frac{1}{4}$.

We call $1\frac{1}{4}$ a mixed number because it includes a whole number part and a fraction part.

Key words
- mixed number
- improper fraction
- simplest form

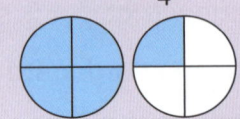

I drew this diagram to show $\frac{5}{4}$.

Draw a diagram to show each of these improper fractions. Write each improper fraction as a mixed number.

1 $\frac{9}{4} = \boxed{}$

4 $\frac{9}{2} = \boxed{}$

Remember: the denominator tells you how many equal parts one whole is divided into.

2 $\frac{11}{3} = \boxed{}$

5 $\frac{7}{6} = \boxed{}$

3 $\frac{15}{4} = \boxed{}$

6 $\frac{18}{5} = \boxed{}$

Stretch zone

Draw a diagram to show an improper fraction between $2\frac{1}{2}$ and $2\frac{3}{4}$.

■ For more practice, go to Practice Book 6, page 55.

3B Mixed numbers and improper fractions

Explore

Mixed number problems

1 Solve these problems.

   a Iona and Alex share three pizzas equally.
   How much pizza does each girl get?

   b Eva and Yvette arrive. They decide to share
   the three pizzas equally between all four girls.
   How much pizza does each girl get now?

2 Jian buys 5 small cakes for himself and his family. He divides
each cake into thirds.

The family members take it in turns to eat some cake. The
table below shows how much cake everyone eats.

Complete the table to find out how much cake is left for Jian.

	Number of cakes eaten	Number of cakes left
	None	5
Dad	$1\frac{1}{3}$	$3\frac{2}{3}$
Mum	$1\frac{2}{3}$	
Big brother	$\frac{2}{3}$	
Big sister	$\frac{2}{3}$	
Jian		

3 Choose your own numbers and fractions and complete this story.

Jian buys ☐ small cakes for himself and his family.

He divides each cake into _____.

Dad eats ☐ cakes. There are ☐ cakes left.

Mum eats ☐ cakes. There are ☐ cakes left.

Big brother eats ☐ cakes. There are ☐ cakes left.

Big sister eats ☐ cakes. There are ☐ cakes left.

Jian eats the rest. Jian eats ☐ cakes.

You can draw the cakes
in your notebook to help
you write the story.

Explore (continued)

4 Three people are eating flatbreads. They eat $\frac{3}{4}$ of a flatbread each.

How many flatbreads do they eat in total?

Write your answers as mixed numbers.

5 Five people are eating pizzas. They eat $\frac{1}{2}$ of a pizza each.

How many pizzas do they eat in total?

6 Two people are eating small cakes. They eat $1\frac{1}{2}$ cakes each.

How many cakes do they eat in total?

Show your workings.

7 Seven people are eating cookies. They eat $\frac{1}{3}$ of a cookie each.

How many cookies do they eat in total?

Stretch zone

Draw a diagram to show each of these fractions:

- a mixed number between $1\frac{1}{2}$ and 3
- an improper fraction smaller than 5
- an improper fraction larger than $3\frac{3}{4}$
- a mixed number smaller than $1\frac{3}{4}$.

62

■ For more practice, go to Practice Book 6, page 56.

Discover

Compare fractions on a number line

Think back

When we compare improper fractions and mixed numbers, it is easier if we convert them to either all mixed numbers or all improper fractions.

Mark each fraction and mixed number on the number line. Circle the fraction that is closer to 1.

Worked example

$1\frac{3}{5}$ and $\frac{7}{10}$

We know that $1\frac{3}{5}$ is the same as $\frac{8}{5}$, which is equivalent to $\frac{16}{10}$.

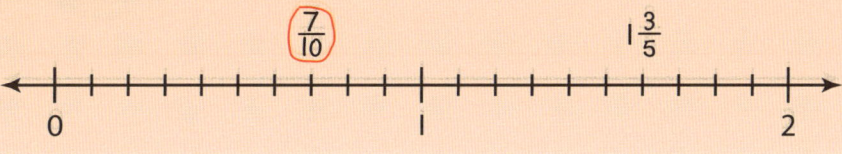

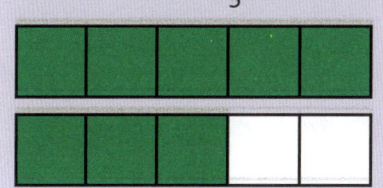

I drew this bar model to show $1\frac{3}{5}$.

The bar model helps me to convert $1\frac{3}{5}$ to $\frac{8}{5}$.

1 $\frac{5}{8}$ and $1\frac{1}{4}$

2 $\frac{3}{4}$ and $1\frac{3}{8}$

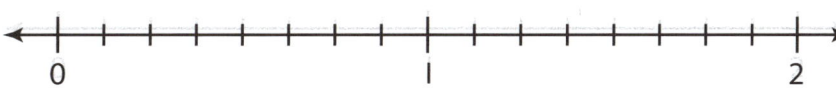

3 $\frac{9}{10}$ and $1\frac{2}{5}$

4 $\frac{8}{10}$ and $1\frac{1}{5}$

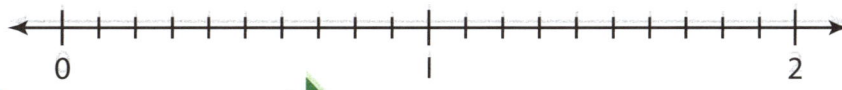

Stretch zone

Choose three fractions. Write them on a number line. Two of the fractions must be greater than 1. Write them as mixed numbers and improper fractions.

■ For more practice, go to Practice Book 6, page 57.

Explore

Key words
- mixed number
- improper fraction
- numerator
- denominator

Order fractions on a number line

Draw number lines to help you order each set of mixed numbers and improper fractions.

- Write the numbers on the number line as both mixed numbers and improper fractions.

Decide which whole numbers to mark on each number line, and what divisions you need.

Worked example

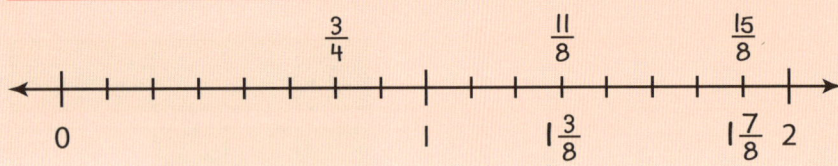

$\frac{3}{4}$ $1\frac{3}{8}$ $1\frac{7}{8}$

1    $\frac{11}{6}$ $2\frac{1}{3}$ $\frac{5}{3}$ $2\frac{1}{6}$

2    $3\frac{1}{2}$ $3\frac{7}{10}$ $\frac{12}{5}$ $3\frac{1}{5}$

3    $5\frac{1}{8}$ $\frac{21}{4}$ $4\frac{7}{8}$ $\frac{9}{2}$

Stretch zone

Draw a number line from $8\frac{1}{2}$ to 9. Mark four mixed numbers on the number line.

■ For more practice, go to Practice Book 6, page 58.

3D Adding and subtracting fractions

Discover

Add and subtract fractions

Key words
- numerator
- denominator
- common multiple
- common denominator

Think back

To add $\frac{3}{4}$ and $\frac{2}{3}$, first make sure that both fractions have the same denominator.

$\frac{3}{4}$ is equivalent to $\frac{9}{12}$ $\frac{2}{3}$ is equivalent to $\frac{8}{12}$

So $\frac{9}{12} + \frac{8}{12} = \frac{17}{12} = 1\frac{5}{12}$

We can also see from the diagram that $\frac{3}{4} - \frac{2}{3} = \frac{1}{12}$

12 is a common multiple of 3 and 4. I can convert both fractions to twelfths.

Draw bar models to help you add and subtract these fractions.

1 $\frac{1}{4} + \frac{5}{12} =$

3 $\frac{3}{4} - \frac{1}{8} =$

2 $\frac{1}{2} + \frac{7}{8} =$

4 $\frac{7}{8} - \frac{1}{2} =$

Stretch zone

Write three addition and subtraction calculations. Each calculation must use fractions with different denominators and have the answer $1\frac{3}{4}$.

■ For more practice, go to Practice Book 6, page 59.

3D Adding and subtracting fractions

Explore

Key words
- numerator
- denominator
- common denominator

Convert fractions to add and subtract

Find the common denominators to help you add and subtract the fractions below.

Worked example

To calculate $1\frac{7}{8} - \frac{3}{4}$, first find a common denominator. We can convert $\frac{3}{4}$ to eighths.

$1\frac{7}{8} - \frac{6}{8}$

It is easier to calculate if we change the mixed number to an improper fraction:

$\frac{15}{8} - \frac{6}{8} = \frac{9}{8}$

Then write the answer as a mixed number: $1\frac{1}{8}$

Write each step of the calculation.

1   $\frac{1}{4} + \frac{7}{12} =$

2   $1\frac{2}{3} + \frac{1}{6} =$

3   $2\frac{1}{6} + \frac{2}{3} =$

4   $3\frac{3}{4} - \frac{1}{2} =$

5   $3\frac{1}{4} - \frac{1}{2} =$

6   $2\frac{3}{4} + \frac{1}{2} =$

7   $3\frac{1}{6} - \frac{1}{3} =$

8   $2\frac{5}{6} - \frac{1}{3} =$

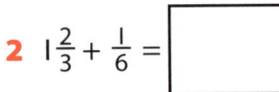 **Stretch zone**

Write an inverse calculation to check each of your answers to **questions 7** and **8**.

■ For more practice, go to Practice Book 6, page 60.

3E Multiplying fractions

Discover

Key words
- numerator
- denominator
- simplest form

Find a fraction of another fraction

Work with a partner.

- Fold a piece of paper into quarters. Roughly shade $\frac{3}{4}$.

- Now fold it into thirds in the opposite direction. Shade $\frac{1}{3}$ in a different colour.

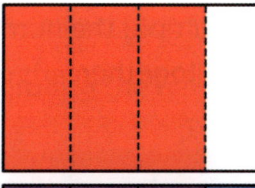

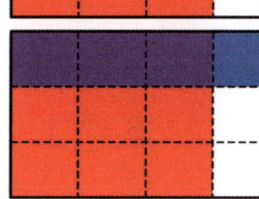

> When we multiply two fractions we can say 'of' instead of 'times'. So $\frac{1}{3}$ of $\frac{3}{4}$ is the same as $\frac{1}{3} \times \frac{3}{4}$.

Fold paper and draw diagrams to help you multiply these fractions.

1 $\frac{1}{3} \times \frac{1}{5} = \boxed{}$

3 $\frac{2}{3} \times \frac{3}{4} = \boxed{}$

2 $\frac{1}{4} \times \frac{1}{2} = \boxed{}$

4 $\frac{1}{4} \times \frac{3}{4} = \boxed{}$

I folded my paper into twelfths. I shaded $\frac{3}{4}$ in red. I shaded $\frac{1}{3}$ in blue. The squares that are both red and blue show $\frac{1}{3}$ of $\frac{3}{4}$. $\frac{1}{3} \times \frac{3}{4} = \frac{3}{12}$

I can write $\frac{3}{12}$ as $\frac{1}{4}$ in its simplest form. $\frac{1}{3} \times \frac{3}{4} = \frac{1}{4}$

Stretch zone

Calculate $\frac{1}{3} \times \frac{1}{5}$, $\frac{1}{3} \times \frac{2}{5}$ and $\frac{1}{3} \times \frac{3}{5}$. What do you notice about your answers?

■ For more practice, go to Practice Book 6, page 61.

3E Multiplying fractions

Explore

Key words
- numerator
- denominator
- simplest form

Multiply two fractions

A quick way to multiply fractions is to multiply the numerators together and multiply the denominators together.

> **Worked example**
>
> Multiply the numerators: $1 \times 3 = 3$
>
> $$\frac{1}{3} \times \frac{3}{4} = \frac{3}{12} = \frac{1}{4}$$
>
> Multiply the denominators: $3 \times 4 = 12$

Remember to give your answer as a fraction in its simplest form. $\frac{3}{12}$ in its simplest form is $\frac{1}{4}$.

1. a $\frac{1}{5} \times \frac{1}{4} = \boxed{}$ b $\frac{1}{5} \times \frac{1}{2} = \boxed{}$ c $\frac{1}{5} \times \frac{3}{4} = \boxed{}$

2. a $\frac{2}{5} \times \frac{1}{4} = \boxed{}$ b $\frac{2}{5} \times \frac{1}{2} = \boxed{}$ c $\frac{2}{5} \times \frac{3}{4} = \boxed{}$

3. a $\frac{3}{5} \times \frac{1}{4} = \boxed{}$ b $\frac{3}{5} \times \frac{1}{2} = \boxed{}$ c $\frac{3}{5} \times \frac{3}{4} = \boxed{}$

4. a $\frac{4}{5} \times \frac{1}{4} = \boxed{}$ b $\frac{4}{5} \times \frac{1}{2} = \boxed{}$ c $\frac{4}{5} \times \frac{3}{4} = \boxed{}$

5. a $\frac{4}{5} \times \frac{1}{5} = \boxed{}$ b $\frac{4}{5} \times \frac{2}{5} = \boxed{}$ c $\frac{4}{5} \times \frac{3}{5} = \boxed{}$

   d $\frac{4}{5} \times \frac{4}{5} = \boxed{}$

6. What patterns do you notice in your answers? Discuss with a partner, then write about what you notice.

_____

_____

_____

_____

Stretch zone

Mariam says, 'When you multiply two numbers together, the answer is always larger than the numbers you multiplied.' Is she correct?

■ For more practice, go to Practice Book 6, page 62.

3F Dividing fractions

Discover

Divide fractions by whole numbers

Key words
- numerator
- denominator
- simplest form
- bar model

1 Use the bar model below to help you with this calculation.

$\frac{1}{2} \div 4 = \boxed{}$

I whole							
	$\frac{1}{2}$				$\frac{1}{2}$		

Can you explain to a partner how this bar model shows $\frac{1}{2} \div 4$?

Draw a bar model to help you with each calculation below.

2 $\frac{1}{3} \div 3 = \boxed{}$

3 Three friends share half a pizza between them. How much of the whole pizza do they each have?

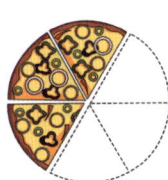

$\frac{1}{2} \div 3 = \boxed{}$

4 I have $\frac{3}{4}$ of a cake left. Anton and I have half each. How much of the whole cake do we each eat?

$\frac{3}{4} \div 2 = \boxed{}$

Stretch zone

Can you write an inverse calculation to check your answer to each question?

3 Fractions, decimals and percentages

■ For more practice, go to Practice Book 6, page 63.

3F Dividing fractions

Explore

Key words
- numerator
- denominator
- simplest form

Use bar models for dividing

Draw bar models to find the answers to these division calculations.

- Write a multiplication calculation to check each answer.

1 $\frac{1}{8} \div 2 =$ ☐

   Multiplication: ☐

2 $\frac{1}{5} \div 2 =$ ☐

   Multiplication: ☐

3 $\frac{1}{6} \div 3 =$ ☐

   Multiplication: ☐

4 $\frac{5}{6} \div 3 =$ ☐

   Multiplication: ☐

5 $\frac{1}{4} \div 3 =$ ☐

   Multiplication: ☐

6 $\frac{3}{4} \div 3 =$ ☐

   Multiplication: ☐

> Explain how the bar models help you with the calculations.

Stretch zone

Arjun says, 'When you divide a number, the answer is always smaller than the number you started with.' Is he correct?

■ For more practice, go to Practice Book 6, page 64.

Discover

Find equivalents

Shade the diagrams to help you find the decimal equivalent of each fraction.

Worked example

$\frac{1}{2}$ [diagram] 0.5

1 $\frac{1}{5}$

2 $\frac{2}{5}$

3 $\frac{1}{4}$

4 $\frac{3}{4}$

5 $\frac{1}{20}$

6 $\frac{1}{25}$

I know that $\frac{1}{2}$ of 10 is 5. I have shaded 5 of the tenths. I write five tenths as 0.5

$\frac{1}{4}$ of 100 is 25. I will shade 25 hundredths. How do I write this as a decimal?

Stretch zone

How can you use your answer to **question 3** to find the decimal equivalent of $\frac{1}{8}$?

3 Fractions, decimals and percentages

71

■ For more practice, go to Practice Book 6, page 65.

3G Fraction and decimal equivalents

Explore

Fraction and decimal problems

1 Complete this table of fraction and decimal equivalents.

Fraction	$\frac{1}{8}$	$\frac{1}{4}$	$\frac{3}{8}$	$\frac{1}{2}$	$\frac{5}{8}$	$\frac{3}{4}$	$\frac{7}{8}$	1
Decimal equivalent	0.125			0.5				1

2 I have 3 bananas and 5 apples.

  a What fraction of the fruit are bananas?

  b Write this as a decimal fraction.

  c What fraction of the fruit are apples?

  d Write this as a decimal fraction.

Use the information in the table to answer these questions.

3 A sports club has 100 balls. 75 are footballs and the rest are basketballs.

  a What fraction of the balls are basketballs?

  b Write this as a decimal fraction.

  c What fraction of the balls are footballs?

  d Write this as a decimal fraction.

Write the fractions in their simplest form.

4 A pizza shop has 40 meat pizzas and 10 vegetarian pizzas.

  a What fraction of the pizzas are vegetarian?

  b Write this as a decimal fraction.

  c What fraction of the pizzas are meat pizzas?

  d Write this as a decimal fraction.

Stretch zone

Write ten more fractions and their decimal equivalents.

■ For more practice, go to Practice Book 6, page 66.

3H Place value in decimals

Discover

Know the value of each digit

| 0 | 1 | 2 | 3 | 4 | 5 | 6 | 7 | 8 | 9 |

Key words
- tenths
- hundredths
- thousandths

1 Follow these steps to make a 6-digit decimal number.

- Pick a card from a set of digit cards 0–9.
- Write the digit in any column in the top row of the place-value grid.
- Replace the card and repeat five more times to complete the top row.

Repeat these steps to make three more 6-digit decimal numbers.

You cannot change the position of your digit at a later stage.

Hundreds	Tens	Ones	•	Tenths	Hundredths	Thousandths
			•			
			•			
			•			
			•			

2 Write numbers following these instructions:

   a the largest number in the grid

   b the largest possible number using the digits from **part a**

   c the smallest number in the grid

   d the smallest possible number using the digits from **part c**

   e the number nearest to 100 in the grid.

Stretch zone

Write any two numbers that have a difference of 5 tenths. Write any two numbers that have a difference of 4 hundredths. Can you explain to a partner how you know you are correct?

■ For more practice, go to Practice Book 6, page 67.

3H Place value in decimals

Explore

Divide by 10, 100 and 1000

1. Choose any 3-digit whole number.

   - Write the number in the first row of the place-value grid.

   Follow these instructions.

   - Divide the number by 10.
   - Write the answer in the next row of the place-value grid.
   - Divide this new number by 10 two more times. Complete the next two rows of the grid.

2. Repeat with two more 3-digit numbers.

	Hundreds	Tens	Ones	•	Tenths	Hundredths	Thousandths
				•			
÷ 10				•			
÷ 10				•			
÷ 10				•			
				•			
÷ 10				•			
÷ 10				•			
÷ 10				•			
				•			
÷ 10				•			
÷ 10				•			
÷ 10				•			

3. Complete these sentences.

   When you divide by 10, the digits move ☐ place to the _____.

   When you divide by 100, _____.

   When you divide by 1000, _____.

Stretch zone

Can you write a general rule for dividing a decimal number by a power of 10?

■ For more practice, go to Practice Book 6, page 68.

31 Multiplying decimals

Discover

Use place-value counters to multiply decimals

We can use place-value counters to represent decimal numbers and decimal calculations.

Worked example

2.313×3

The counters in the grid show 2.313, three times.

Tens	Ones	.	Tenths	Hundredths	Thousandths
	●●	.	●●●	●	●●●
	●●	.	●●●	●	●●●
	●●	.	●●●	●	●●●

The counters show that the answer is 6.939

If I have 10 thousandths, I can exchange these for 1 hundredth.

If I have 10 hundredths, I can exchange these for 1 tenth, and so on.

Use place-value counters and draw them in the boxes below.

1 $3.321 \times 3 = $ ___

3 $4.102 \times 3 = $ ___

2 $3.321 \times 4 = $ ___

4 $5.552 \times 2 = $ ___

Stretch zone

Write a multiplication, with decimals, that **does not** need any exchanges.

Write a multiplication, with decimals, that **does** need exchanges. Which is easier to solve?

■ For more practice, go to Practice Book 6, page 69.

31 Multiplying decimals

Explore

Use a written method to multiply decimals

Samira wrote this calculation.

	2	.	7	2			
×				5			
	0	.	1	0			(5 × 0.02)
	3	.	5	0			(5 × 0.7)
1	0	.	0	0			(5 × 2)
1	3	.	6	0			

Key words
- tenths
- hundredths
- thousandths

> Remember to estimate first. 3 × 5 = 15 so I know the answer should be a bit less than 15.

💬 **1** Talk to a partner. Explain the method that Samira has used.

2 Use this method to work out these multiplications.

a 3.71 × 4

c 5.66 × 4

b 4.28 × 3

d 8.17 × 7

Stretch zone

Rashid says, 'When I multiply a number with two decimal places by a whole number, the answer always has two decimal places.' Is he correct? Write some examples to support your answer.

76

3J Dividing decimals

Discover

Use place-value counters to divide decimals

We can use place-value counters to represent decimal numbers, and decimal calculations.

Key words

- tenths
- hundredths
- thousandths

> **Worked example**
>
> 3.369 ÷ 3
>
> The counters in the place-value grid show 3.369 divided equally into three rows.
>
> | Tens | Ones | . | Tenths | Hundredths | Thousandths |
> |------|------|---|--------|------------|-------------|
> | | 🔴 | . | 🟡 | 🟢🟢 | 🔵🔵🔵 |
> | | 🔴 | . | 🟡 | 🟢🟢 | 🔵🔵🔵 |
> | | 🔴 | . | 🟡 | 🟢🟢 | 🔵🔵🔵 |

1 Complete these sentences about the calculation in the worked example.

3 ones divided by 3 is ☐ ones.

3 tenths divided by 3 is ☐ tenths.

6 hundredths divided by 3 is ☐ hundredths.

9 thousandths divided by 3 is ☐ thousandths.

So, 3.369 ÷ 3 = ☐

2 Use place-value counters and place-value grids to complete these calculations.

a 4.024 ÷ 4 = ☐   **c** 5.452 ÷ 2 = ☐

b 3.975 ÷ 3 = ☐

> Remember: you can exchange 10 counters for 1 counter of the next value. For example, you can exchange 10 thousandths counters for 1 hundredth counter.

Stretch zone

Write a multiplication calculation to check each of your answers.

■ For more practice, go to Practice Book 6, page 71.

3J Dividing decimals

Explore

Use a written method to divide decimals

Victor wrote this calculation.

```
      1 . 3  7
  5 ) 6 . ¹8 ³5
```

Key words
- tenths
- hundredths
- thousandths

Remember to estimate first. $5 \div 5 = 1$ and $10 \div 5 = 2$ so I know the answer will be between 1 and 2.

1 Talk to a partner about Victor's strategy.

First, Victor …

Then, he …

Then, he …

So, the answer is …

2 Use this method to work out these divisions.

a $8.85 \div 5$

c $8.28 \div 4$

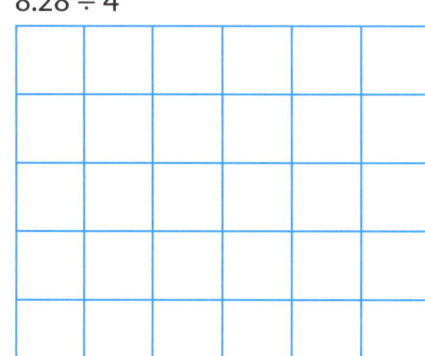

b $9.27 \div 3$

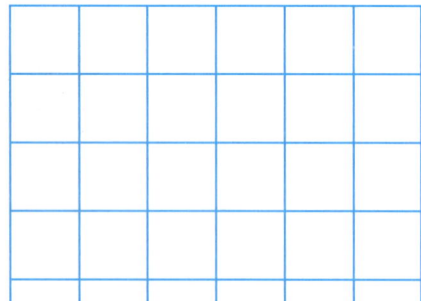

d $12.28 \div 4$

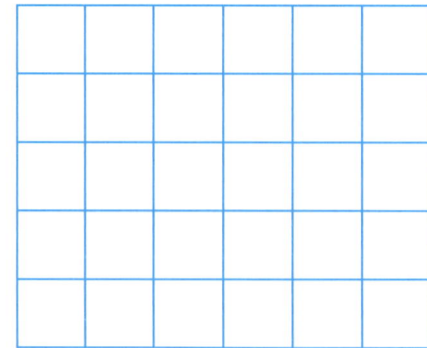

Check your answers by multiplying.

Stretch zone

Faith says, 'When I divide a number with two decimal places by a whole number, the answer always has two decimal places.' Is she correct? Write some examples to support your answer.

78

3K Decimal problems

Discover

Nearest tenth

Pick three cards from a set of digit cards 0–9.

- Make five different 3-digit numbers with two decimal places.
- Use your numbers to complete the sentences below.
- You can draw number lines to help you.

Worked example

3.68 is between 3.6 and 3.7 but nearer to 3.7

3.68 is 3.7 rounded to the nearest tenth.

								↓		
3.6	3.6l	3.62	3.63	3.64	3.65	3.66	3.67	3.68	3.69	**3.7**

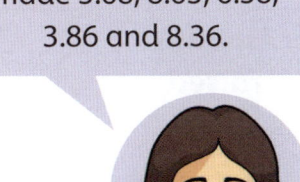

I picked 3, 6 and 8 and made 3.68, 8.63, 6.38, 3.86 and 8.36.

1. [ ] is between [ ] and [ ] but nearer to [ ].

   [ ] is [ ] rounded to the nearest tenth.

2. [ ] is between [ ] and [ ] but nearer to [ ].

   [ ] is [ ] rounded to the nearest tenth.

3. [ ] is between [ ] and [ ] but nearer to [ ].

   [ ] is [ ] rounded to the nearest tenth.

4. [ ] is between [ ] and [ ] but nearer to [ ].

   [ ] is [ ] rounded to the nearest tenth.

5. [ ] is between [ ] and [ ] but nearer to [ ].

   [ ] is [ ] rounded to the nearest tenth.

Rounding to the nearest tenth is the same as rounding to one decimal place (I d.p.).

Stretch zone

Write three pairs of numbers that have a difference of three thousandths.

3 Fractions, decimals and percentages

■ For more practice, go to Practice Book 6, page 73.

3K Decimal problems

Explore

Charity donations

Business A tells a charity that it will donate double the amount of money that the charity raises each week.

Over five weeks the charity raised the amounts shown in the table.

Use your knowledge of multiplying and dividing decimals to solve these problems.

Week	Week 1	Week 2	Week 3	Week 4	Week 5
Amount raised	$28.73	$32.54	$16.76	$58.62	$63.48
Amount donated by Business A					

1 Complete the table to show how much Business A donated.

2 What is the total amount donated?

Business B says that it will round up the amount that the charity raises each week to the next $10 and donate double the rounded amount.

3 Complete this table to show how much Business B donated.

Week	Week 1	Week 2	Week 3	Week 4	Week 5
Amount raised	$28.73	$32.54	$16.76	$58.62	$63.48
Amount donated by Business B					

Business B always rounds up, not down, even if the amount is closer to a lower multiple of $10.

4 What is the total amount donated?

Stretch zone

How much extra money did Business B donate by doubling the rounded amounts rather than doubling the actual amounts?

80

3L Fractions, decimals and percentages

Discover

Fraction and percentage equivalents

1 Shade the percentage of each circle.

a 20% **b** 40% **c** 75%

2 The total number of marks in a test is 80. The table shows some possible marks out of 80.

● Complete the table to show the equivalent percentage scores.

Marks out of 80	Fraction	Fraction in its simplest form	Percentage
80			100%
70			
60			
55			
45			
40			
20			
10			
8			10%
4			
2			
1			
0			0%

What fractions will you divide each circle into, in order to shade the correct percentage?

I got 70 out of 80 marks. That is $\frac{70}{80}$ or $\frac{7}{8}$ in its simplest form.

For the percentages that you don't know, add together percentages that you do know.

 **Stretch zone**

Usman achieved 57.5% in the test. How many marks did he get?

■ For more practice, go to Practice Book 6, page 75.

3 Fractions, decimals and percentages

Explore

Fraction, decimal and percentage equivalents

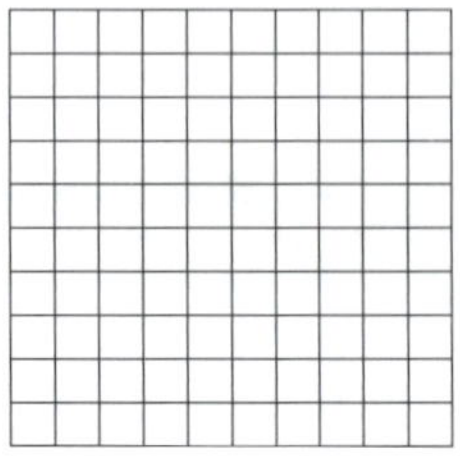

Key words
- fraction
- decimal
- percentage
- equivalent

I Complete this table.

- Write the decimal and percentage equivalent of each fraction.
- Shade the 100-square to show the percentage.

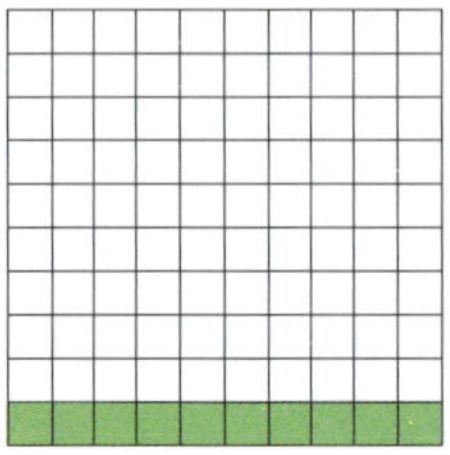

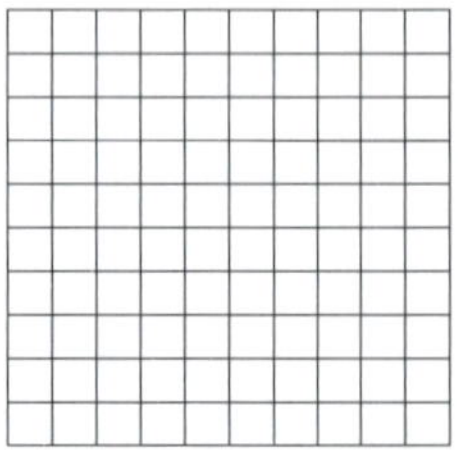

Fraction	Decimal / Percentage	100-square
$\frac{1}{10}$	$=$ 0.1 $=$ 10 %	
$\frac{3}{5}$	$=$ ☐ $=$ ☐ %	
$\frac{1}{5}$	$=$ ☐ $=$ ☐ %	
$\frac{7}{10}$	$=$ ☐ $=$ ☐ %	
$\frac{1}{4}$	$=$ ☐ $=$ ☐ %	
$\frac{3}{4}$	$=$ ☐ $=$ ☐ %	
$\frac{3}{10}$	$=$ ☐ $=$ ☐ %	
$\frac{4}{5}$	$=$ ☐ $=$ ☐ %	
$\frac{2}{5}$	$=$ ☐ $=$ ☐ %	
I whole	$=$ ☐ $=$ ☐ %	
$\frac{1}{2}$	$=$ ☐ $=$ ☐ %	
$\frac{1}{100}$	$=$ ☐ $=$ ☐ %	

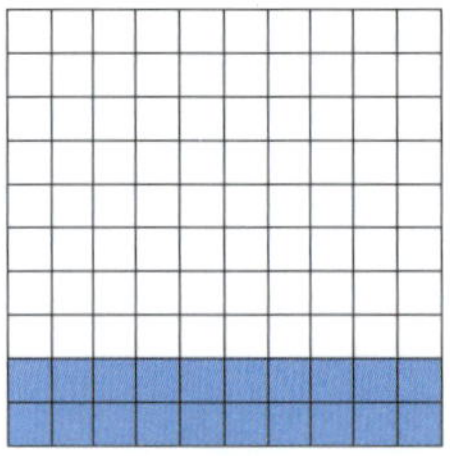

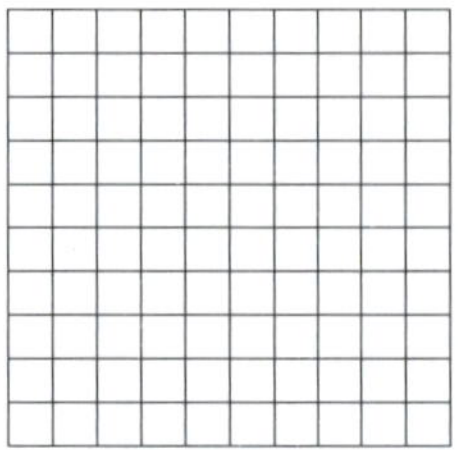

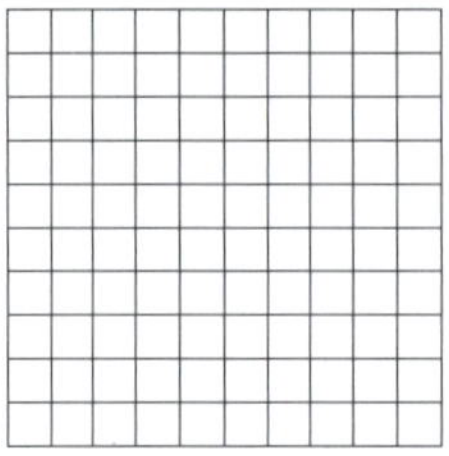

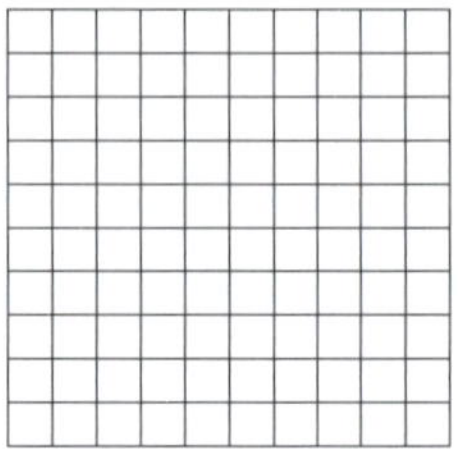

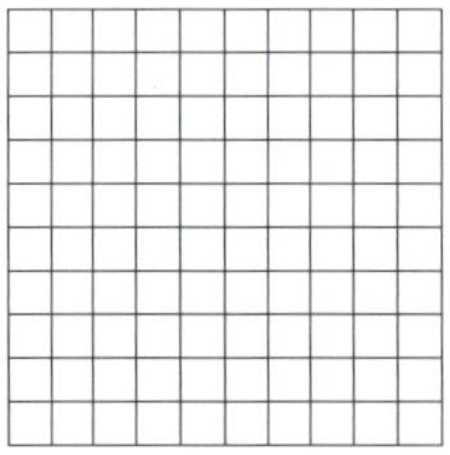

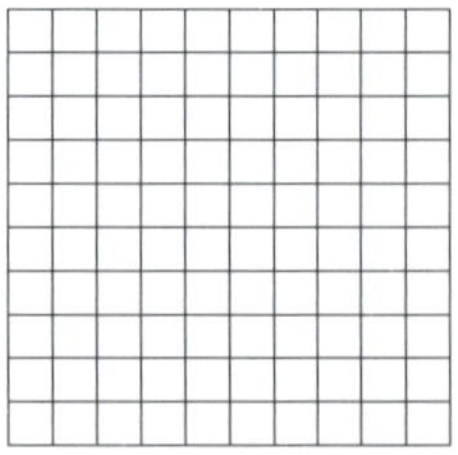

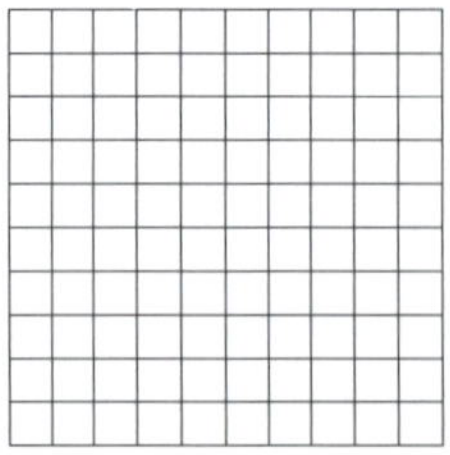

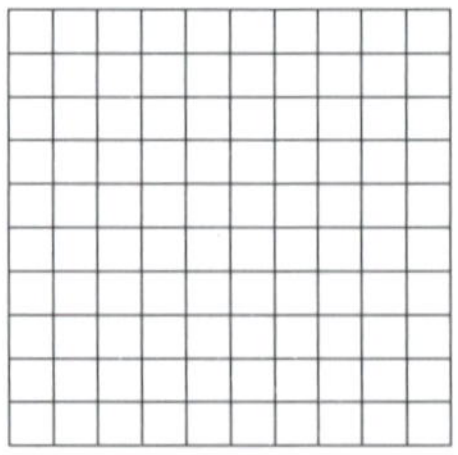

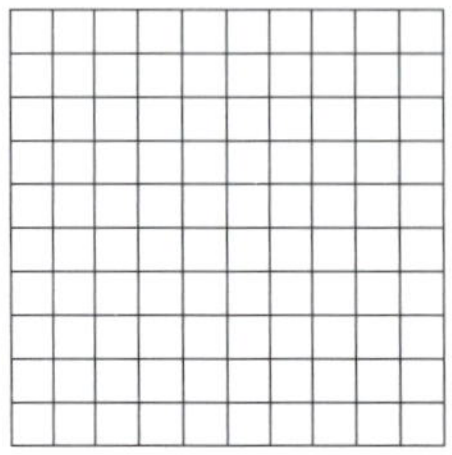

Explore (continued)

2 Copy and complete this table on a piece of paper or card.

- Cut the cards out and shuffle them.
- Use the cards to play the memory game with your partner.

	$\frac{1}{5}$	0.2	
	$\frac{2}{5}$	0.4	40%
	$\frac{1}{2}$		50%
	$\frac{3}{5}$		60%
	$\frac{7}{10}$	0.7	70%
	$\frac{3}{4}$	0.75	
		0.8	80%

Stretch zone

Add two more sets of cards of your own to the game. Try to make them as challenging as possible.

■ For more practice, go to Practice Book 6, page 76.

3 Fractions, decimals and percentages

Connect

Clothes shop sale prices

Work in a group. Imagine you own a clothes shop. You sell the following items.

Item	Usual selling price	Cost price
T-shirt	$6	$2
Shorts	$8	$3
Jeans	$14	$10
Sandals	$5	$2

You reduce the selling price of the items in a sale. You must reduce:

- one item by 10%
- one item by a quarter
- one item by 15%
- one item by a half.

You usually sell these items in the following proportions.

Item	Percentage sales
T-shirts	40%
Shorts	30%
Jeans	20%
Sandals	10%

The difference between the cost price and the selling price is called the margin. The greater the margin, the more money you will make.

In order to make the most money, you need to decide which item to reduce by each percentage.

Write the percentage reductions and the new prices here.

Think about how reducing the selling price will affect the margin.

Item	% reduction	Sale price
T-shirt	☐ %	$ ☐
Shorts	☐ %	$ ☐
Jeans	☐ %	$ ☐
Sandals	☐ %	$ ☐

Stretch zone

Write a presentation to explain your decisions to your class.

3 Fractions, decimals and percentages

Review

1 Write the missing number to make this division correct.

$0.2 \div \boxed{} = 0.02$

2 Choose a symbol to make each statement correct.

$$\boxed{< \qquad > \qquad =}$$

a $\dfrac{3}{10}$ $\boxed{}$ 0.03

b $\dfrac{3}{4}$ $\boxed{}$ 0.8

c 0.125 $\boxed{}$ $\dfrac{1}{4}$

d 60% $\boxed{}$ $\dfrac{2}{3}$

e $\dfrac{3}{4}$ $\boxed{}$ 75%

f 12.5% $\boxed{}$ 0.15

3 Circle the fractions that are equal to 0.8

$\dfrac{4}{5}$ $\qquad$ $\dfrac{1}{8}$ $\qquad$ $\dfrac{10}{8}$ $\qquad$ $\dfrac{8}{10}$ $\qquad$ $\dfrac{8}{5}$

4 A box of five toy cars costs $5.72.
How much will 15 cars cost?

$\boxed{}$

5 Circle the fractions and decimals that are between $1\frac{1}{2}$ and 2.

1.75 $\qquad$ 2.001 $\qquad$ $\dfrac{9}{5}$ $\qquad$ $\dfrac{15}{4}$ $\qquad$ $\dfrac{7}{4}$

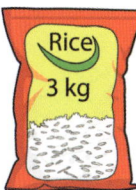

6 Rice costs $3.98 per kilogram. Chicken costs $4.85 per kilogram.
How much do 3 kg of rice and 5 kg of chicken cost?

In this unit you will:

- solve problems using ratio and proportion
- use your knowledge of factors and multiples to solve problems
- solve problems using percentages
- use scale factors to solve problems.

?

How do I use scale factors and ratio and proportion to solve everyday problems?

Engage

Kiara is going on holiday for 10 days. These are the items that she is taking.

The ratio of T-shirts to pairs of socks is 5 : 10 That is the same as 1 : 2

So, Kiara has twice as many pairs of socks as T-shirts.

There are 30 items in Kiara's case. $\frac{10}{30}$ or $\frac{1}{3}$ of the items are pairs of socks!

What other ratios, proportions and fractions can you see?

4A Ratio

Discover

Mixing paint

Key words
- ratio
- one to four (1 : 4)

You can mix different amounts of blue and yellow paint to make different shades of green.

Paint A and Paint B are in tins of the same size.

Paint A is a mixture of blue and yellow paint in the ratio 1 : 4

Paint B is a mixture of blue and yellow paint in the ratio 2 : 3

Paint A   Paint B

> Paint A is a mixture of 1 part blue paint to 4 parts yellow paint.
>
> The ratio of yellow to blue paint is 4 : 1

Worked example

I need to use one tin of paint A and two tins of paint B. I can draw a diagram to show the ratios in each paint tin.

Paint A

Paint B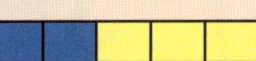

Paint B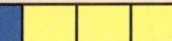

This gives a total ratio of blue to yellow paint of 5 : 10 or 1 : 2

> Draw diagrams like the one in the worked example to help you find the different ratios.

 Investigate the different ratios of blue to yellow paint you can make using different numbers of tins of Paint A and Paint B.

Stretch zone

Present your findings to the rest of the class. Did you all find the same ratios? What was the same? What was different?

■ For more practice, go to Practice Book 6, page 78.

4A Ratio

Explore

Ratio problems

I Kabir is tiling a floor using this pattern of tiles.

The pattern has one black tile for every two white tiles.

Kabir's room is 6 tiles wide and 12 tiles long.

a Write the ratio of black tiles to white tiles.

☐ : ☐

b How many black tiles does he need? ☐

c How many white tiles does he need? ☐

d Kabir buys 39 tiles in the correct ratio.

How many white tiles does he buy? ☐

2 To make a fruit drink for three people, Rafael mixes fruit juice and water in the ratio of I part fruit juice to 3 parts water. This makes 200 millilitres of fruit drink.

a Write the ratio of fruit juice to water.

☐ : ☐

b How much fruit juice does Rafael need for six people? ☐ ml

c How much water does Rafael need to mix with 150 millilitres of fruit juice?

☐ ml

Stretch zone

Zainab makes lemonade drinks in two glasses. One glass has 150 ml water and 100 ml lemonade. The other has 100 ml water and 75 ml lemonade.
Which tastes more strongly of lemonade? Explain how your knowledge of ratios helps you to solve this problem.

■ For more practice, go to Practice Book 6, page 79.

4B Proportion

Discover

Proportion problems

There are 24 girls and 12 boys in Hugo's class. If the students stand in an array, you can see that the ratio of girls to boys is 2 : 1.

You can also see that $\frac{2}{3}$ of the class are girls. We say the proportion of students that are girls is $\frac{2}{3}$.

I always get confused between ratio and proportion. Can you explain the difference?

1   Talk to a partner, then complete the following sentence.

The difference between ratio and proportion is

_____

_____

2   There are 16 yellow flowers and 4 blue flowers in a flower bed.

   a   What is the ratio of yellow flowers to blue flowers?

   b   What proportion of the flowers are yellow?

3   Camille makes a pattern with cubes. There are 30 cubes altogether. Five are green and the rest are red.

   a   What is the ratio or red cubes to green cubes?

   b   What proportion of the cubes are red?

4   A shop sells bananas and mangos. There are 55 bananas and 45 mangos.

   a   What is the ratio of bananas to mangos?

   b   What proportion of the fruit are mangos?

 **Stretch zone**

Write the proportions in these questions as percentages and as decimal fractions.

■ For more practice, go to Practice Book 6, page 80.

4B Proportion

Explore

Proportions as fractions and percentages

Think back

We can write proportion as a fraction, a percentage or as a decimal fraction.

1 Oliver says, 'There are three coloured pencils for every pen in my pencil case. This means that $\frac{1}{3}$ of the items in my pencil case are pens.'

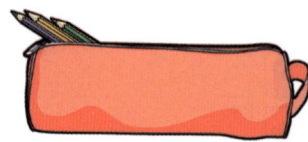

Draw a diagram to show why Oliver is incorrect.

Draw diagrams, such as bar models, to help you with these problems.

2 There are 80 flowers in a bed. $\frac{2}{5}$ of the flowers are red and the rest are yellow. How many flowers of each colour are there?

a Red [   ]   **b** Yellow [   ]

3 I use 150 counters in a pattern. $\frac{1}{3}$ of the counters are green and the rest are blue. How many counters of each colour are there?

a Green [   ]   **b** Blue [   ]

4 There are 30 students in a class. 60% are boys and the rest are girls. How many girls and boys are there in the class?

a Boys [   ]   **b** Girls [   ]

5 There are 1200 trees in a forest. $\frac{1}{6}$ are palm trees and the rest are cypress trees. How many of each type of tree are there?

a Palm trees [   ]   **b** Cypress trees [   ]

Stretch zone

Write a proportion word problem for a partner to solve.

■ For more practice, go to Practice Book 6, page 81.

4C Percentage problems

Discover

Election percentages

The table shows the results in last year's local election.

 Candidate A    Candidate B    Candidate C    Candidate D

Candidate	Number of votes	Percentage of votes (to the nearest whole number)
A	1525	
B	2750	
C	858	
D	1899	
Total votes	7032	

1 Complete the table.

2 Each candidate paid a deposit to stand in the election. A candidate loses this deposit if they get less than 15% of the votes. Did any candidates lose their deposit?

_____

3 In this year's election, candidate A's votes increased by 24%. Candidate B's votes decreased by 17%. Did candidate A or B receive more votes in this year's election?

4 Candidate C did not stand in this year's election. All the 858 voters who voted for candidate C last year voted for candidate D instead. What is the percentage increase in the votes for candidate D?

Stretch zone

Find a newspaper headline that uses percentages. Check that it is accurate.

■ For more practice, go to Practice Book 6, page 82.

Key words
- percentage increase
- percentage decrease

To find 1525 as a percentage of the total number of votes, I first divide 1525 by the total number of votes. Then I multiply the answer by 100%.

Use a calculator and round each percentage to the nearest whole number.

4 Ratio and proportion

4C Percentage problems

Explore

Tax percentage problems

Many items that you buy include sales tax. This amount varies from country to country. For example, sales tax is:

How can you use some of the rows to help you complete the other rows in the table?

| 20% in the UK | | 10% in Australia | | 18% in Peru |

1 Find out the sales tax in your country.

In _____ the sales tax is [   ] %.

2 Complete this table.

Price before tax	Total cost with 20% tax	Total cost with 10% tax	Total cost with 18% tax	Total cost in your country with tax
$25				
$30				
$50				
$75				
$125				
$250				

Stretch zone

Why do you think that the sales tax is different in different countries?

■ For more practice, go to Practice Book 6, page 83.

4D Scaling problems

Key words
- scale factor
- ratio
- enlarge
- enlargement

Discover

Shape scale drawings

You will need centimetre-squared paper for this activity.

1 Draw these shapes on your paper, following these instructions.

- Draw the arrow double the size of the one below.
- Draw the rectangle 3 times larger than the one below.
- Draw the triangle 4 times larger than the one below.

When you enlarge a shape, multiply all the side lengths by the scale factor.

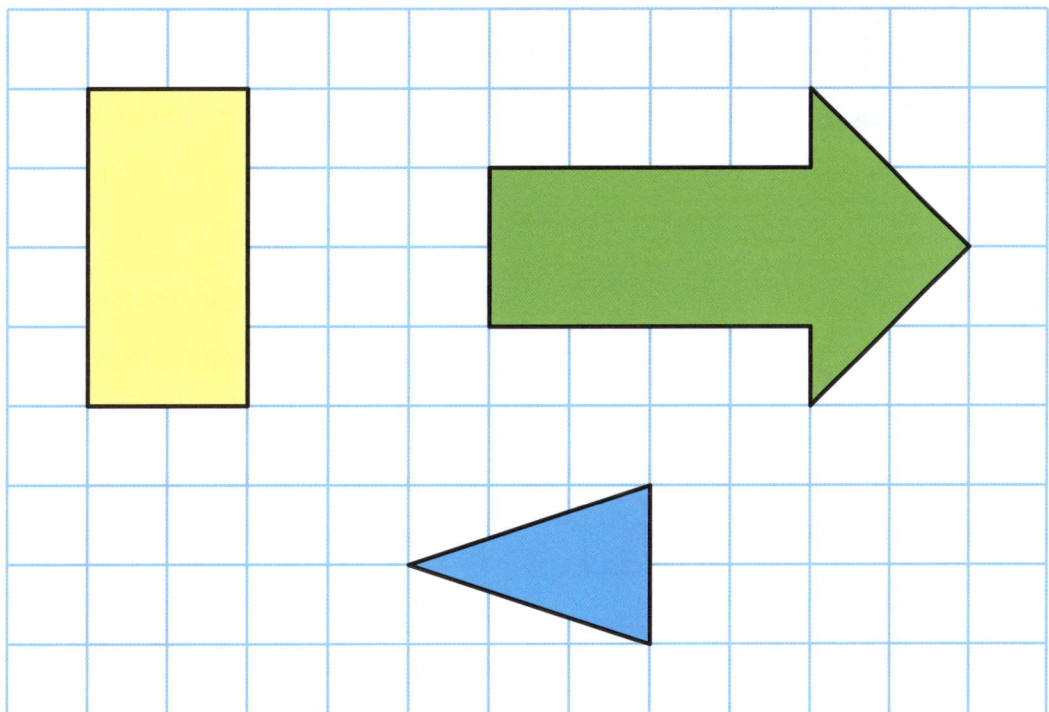

2 Draw a rectangle that measures 2.5 cm by 6 cm.

- Now enlarge the rectangle by a scale factor of 3.

3 Draw an equilateral triangle with side lengths of 4.5 cm.

- Now enlarge the triangle by a scale factor of 2.

4 Draw any simple shape that you like. Give it to a partner to enlarge by a scale factor of 4. The enlargement must fit on the paper!

Stretch zone

Sobia says, 'If you double the side lengths of a rectangle, you double the area.' Is she correct? Justify your answer.

 For more practice, go to Practice Book 6, page 84.

4D Scaling problems

Explore

Recipe scaling problem

Here are the ingredients to make chicken curry for 12 people.

Key words
- scale factor
- ratio

Ingredients

6 onions

150 ml oil

750 g chicken

3 tins of tomatoes

240 g lentils

1 ½ tbsp mixed spices

1 Write the list of ingredients for 4 people.

_____   _____

_____   _____

_____   _____

How will you reduce the recipe from 12 portions to 4 portions? Use the same scale factor for each of the ingredients.

2 I bought all the ingredients shown in the recipe, but I have $1\frac{1}{2}$ tins of tomatoes left over. How many people have I cooked for?

3 I use 500 g of chicken. How many people have I cooked for?

4 I have 20 onions and lots of the other ingredients. How many people can I cook for?

5 Write the list of ingredients for 16 people.

_____   _____

_____   _____

_____   _____

 Stretch zone

Write the ingredients for your favourite recipe in your notebook. Make up some scaling problems for a partner to solve, using your recipe ingredients.

■ For more practice, go to Practice Book 6, page 85.

4 Ratio and proportion

Connect

Classroom scale drawing

🗨 Work as a group on this activity.

Make a scale drawing of your classroom.

- Measure the classroom and all the furniture.
- Then decide on the scale factor so your drawing will fit onto the grid below.
- Write the scale you have used.

> Plan your drawing first on a large piece of squared paper.

Scale:

💡 **I can solve everyday problems using scale factors, ratio and proportion. I often use my knowledge of fractions and of multiplication and division.**

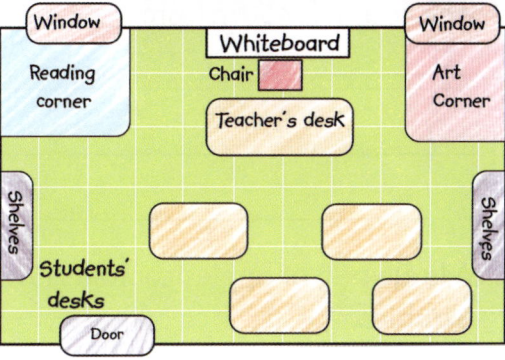

Stretch zone

How big will each item of furniture be if you increase it by a scale factor of 6 from the original size?

4 Ratio and proportion

Review

1 It is 900 m from point A to point C. The distance from B to C is twice the distance from A to B.

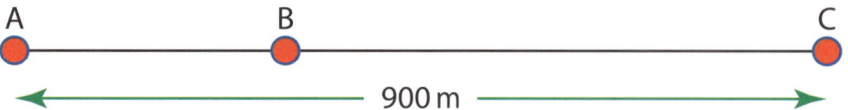

Ana says it is 450 m from B to C. Explain why she is not correct.

_____

_____

_____

2 A large bag of apples contains 16 apples. A small bag contains 6 apples.

a How can I buy exactly 44 apples? _____

_____

b How can I buy exactly 40 apples? _____

_____

3 Lena is making a scale drawing of her classroom. The classroom is 15 m long and 5 m wide. Lena uses the scale 1 cm : 50 cm. What size paper does she need for her scale drawing?

_____

4 Karl has £450. He uses 75% of his money to buy a mountain bike. How much money does he have left?

$ [ ]

5 Zara plants some seeds in her garden. For every 5 seeds that she plants, only 3 grow. 15 plants grow. How many seeds did Zara plant?

[ ]

5 Algebra

In this unit you will:

- use simple formulae
- generate and describe linear number sequences
- solve missing number problems
- solve equations with unknown values
- solve problems with variables.

?

What sort of problems can I solve using algebra?

I use a formula to find volumes too.

Engage

I use a formula to work out the areas of shapes.

I know that the area of a rectangle is length × width.

I know that the area of a triangle is $\frac{1}{2}$ (base × height).

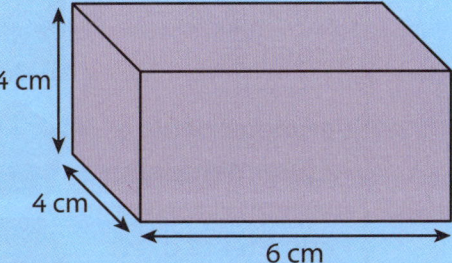

4 cm

4 cm

6 cm

4 cm

8 cm

5 cm

6 cm

Area of a rectangle = $l \times w$

8 cm × 4 cm

= 32 cm²

Area of a triangle = $\frac{1}{2} b \times h$

$\frac{1}{2} \times 6$ cm × 5 cm

= 15 cm²

Volume of a cuboid = $l \times w \times h$

6 cm × 4 cm × 4 cm

= 96 cm³

I use a formula when I am cooking.

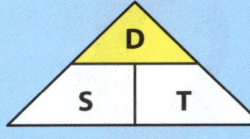
Distance = Speed × Time

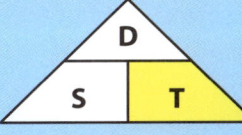
Time = $\dfrac{\text{Distance}}{\text{Speed}}$

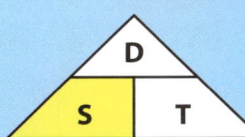
Speed = $\dfrac{\text{Distance}}{\text{Time}}$

I use a formula to work out how long it will take me to get somewhere.

25 min per 450 g + 25 min

5A Number sequences

Discover

Key word
- linear number sequence

Shape number sequences

Think back

Perimeter means the distance around the outside of a shape.

Investigate the perimeters of some regular shapes.

1 Complete this table.

Side length	1 cm	2 cm	3 cm	4 cm	5 cm	6 cm
Perimeter of an equilateral triangle						
Perimeter of a square						
Perimeter of a regular pentagon						
Perimeter of a regular hexagon						

2 What do you notice about the number patterns as you move down the rows? _____

_____

3 What do you notice about the number patterns as you move across the columns? _____

_____

4 Can you explain why these patterns are formed?

_____

_____

Why do you think these number sequences are called **linear** sequences?

Stretch zone

Investigate the patterns formed by the perimeters of regular octagons and decagons. First, try to predict the patterns. Then work out the perimeters to find out if you were correct.

■ For more practice, go to Practice Book 6, page 87.

5A Number sequences

Explore

Rules for number sequences

1 Complete the linear number sequence in each table.

- Below each table, write the rule for generating the next number of the sequence.

Worked example

Term	1	2	3	4	5	6	7
Number	$\frac{1}{4}$	1	$1\frac{3}{4}$	$2\frac{1}{2}$			

The rule is ___add $\frac{3}{4}$_____

a

Term	1	2	3	4	5	6	7
Number	55	25	$^-5$				

The rule is _____

b

Term	1	2	3	4	5	6	7
Number	0.8	1.6	2.4				

The rule is _____

2 Write your own sequences in these tables, but do not write the rules yet.

- Give your sequences to a partner . Ask your partner to complete each sequence and write the rule.

a

Term	1	2	3	4	5	6	7
Number							

The rule is _____

b

Term	1	2	3	4	5	6	7
Number							

The rule is _____

Key words
- linear number sequence
- rule
- term

Look at any two consecutive numbers. What is the difference between them?

Is the difference between consecutive numbers always the same in every number sequence?

Explore (continued)

3 Lu made a sequence using pencils.

> Use pencils or toothpicks to help you.
>
>

a Count the pencils and complete the table.

Shape number	1	2	3	4	5	6
Number of pencils	4	7	10			

b What is the rule for the number of pencils in this sequence?

_____

c How many pencils will be in the 10th shape?

d How many pencils will be in the 20th shape?

4 Here are the first two shapes in another sequence.

a Complete the table for this sequence.

Shape number	1	2	3	4	5	6
Number of pencils						

b What is the rule for the number of pencils in this sequence?

_____

c How many pencils will be in the 10th shape?

d How many pencils will be in the 20th shape?

Stretch zone

Make up your own sequence using pencils and write the number sequence that it generates.

100

■ For more practice, go to Practice Book 6, page 88.

5B Using a formula

Discover

Rectangle formulae

Key words
- formula/formulae
- unknown
- variable
- constant

Think back

The formula for finding the perimeter of a rectangle is:

$P = 2w + 2l$

l = length
w = width
P = perimeter

$P = w + l + w + l$
$P = 2w + 2l$

Another way of writing this formula is: $P = 2(w + l)$

You add the width and length together, and then double the total.

1 Write the formula for the *area* of a rectangle.

2 Use the two formulae to investigate the areas and perimeters of rectangles with the following dimensions. Complete the table.

Rectangle dimensions (cm)	10 × 10	10 × 12	12 × 12	12 × 14	14 × 14	14 × 16	16 × 16	16 × 18
Perimeter (cm)								
Area (cm²)								

3 Describe any patterns that you can see in the table.

_____

_____

_____

Stretch zone

Think about other irregular shapes that you know (for example, rhombus, parallelogram). Write the formula for finding the perimeter of each shape. How are the formulae the same? How are they different?

5 Algebra

101

For more practice, go to Practice Book 6, page 89.

5B Using a formula

Explore

Distance, time, speed formulae

This triangle shows how to make the formulae for calculating speed, time and distance.

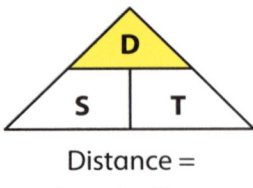 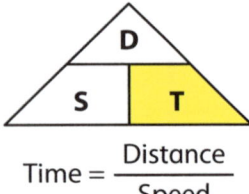 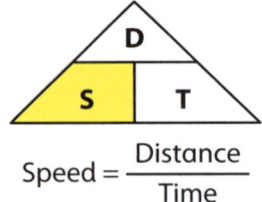

Distance = Speed × Time

$$Time = \frac{Distance}{Speed}$$

$$Speed = \frac{Distance}{Time}$$

Key words
- formula/formulae
- unknown
- variable
- constant
- kilometres per hour (kph)

In a formula, a horizontal bar means divide. For example:
$$\frac{Distance}{Speed}$$
means Distance ÷ Speed.

 Use the distance, time and speed formulae to solve these problems. Use your notebook for your workings.

1 I walk at a speed of 5 kilometres per hour (5 kph) for 2 hours. How far do I walk? 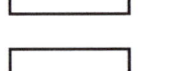 km

2 I cycle at a speed of 15 kph for 2 hours. How far do I travel?  km

3 I drive at a speed of 45 kph for 2 hours. How far do I travel?  km

4 How long does it take me to walk 10 km at a speed of 5 kph?  hours

5 How long does it take me to cycle 10 km at a speed of 15 kph? 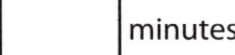 minutes

6 How long does it take me to drive 10 km at a speed of 60 kph? 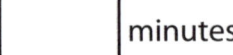 minutes

7 I walk 12 km in 3 hours. What is my walking speed?  kph

8 I cycle 10 km in half an hour. What is my cycling speed?  kph

9 I drive 100 km in 2 hours. What is my driving speed? kph

If I know two of the values, I can find the third one.

Stretch zone

What do you notice about the patterns in the answers?

 102

■ For more practice, go to Practice Book 6, page 90.

5C Missing number problems

Discover

Key words
- equation
- missing number
- unknown

Use algebra to find unknown numbers

1 Look at this table. Work out the value of each shape.

a

b

c

●●●	$3c = 9$
■■	$2s = 8$
■●	$s + c = 7$
■▲●	$s + t + c = 14$

> We can use a letter to represent each shape and use the letters to write equations. For example, $3c = 9$ means that the value of 3 circles is 9.

> When I know the values of all the shapes, I can replace the letters with the correct numbers.

2 Now choose your own value for each shape.

- Write the values in your notebook and do not show them to your partner.
- Write an equation using algebra in each row of the table. Check your equations to make sure they are correct.

	Algebraic equation
●●●	
■■	
■▲	
▲●●	
●▲■	

> I decide the circle has a value of 9. In the first row, I write the algebraic equation $3c = 27$.

- Swap your table with a partner. Ask your partner to work out the value of each shape.

Stretch zone

Choose a new value for each shape. Write equations using letters for the unknown values. Give your equations to a partner to solve.

5 Algebra

103

■ For more practice, go to Practice Book 6, page 91.

5C Missing number problems

Explore

Use algebra to solve problems

Worked example

Jing spends $9 on a magazine and a book.

The book costs $6.45 but she does not remember how much the magazine costs. She writes:

magazine + book = $9

magazine + $6.45 = $9

To work out the cost of the magazine, Jing works out $9 – $6.45

So, magazine = $2.55

You can write the equation using algebra. I used the letter m instead of the word 'magazine'.

$$m + 6.45 = 9$$
$$m = 9 - 6.45$$
$$m = 2.55$$

Write equations and then solve them to find the answers to these problems.

1 I spend $15 on some cherries and some apples. The cherries cost $8.75. How much do the apples cost?

2 A rectangle has an area of 28 cm². It is 4 cm wide. How long is it?

You can also draw a bar model. For example:

$9	
	$6.45

3 Mya walks to visit Sophie and Odette. It takes her 35 minutes to walk to Sophie's house. Mya walks for 95 minutes altogether. How long does it take her to walk to Odette's house?

4 I read 45 pages of my book on Monday, starting at page 1. On Tuesday I finished on page 76. How many pages did I read on Tuesday?

5 Pierce has 75 stickers. He gives some to Ramón. Pierce has 49 stickers left. How many does he give to Ramón?

Stretch zone

Write a word problem for this equation: $a - 23 = 65$

■ For more practice, go to Practice Book 6, page 92.

5D Problems with two unknowns

Discover

Numbers of animals in a zoo

In a zoo, there are some emus and some zebras.

I can see 24 heads and 66 legs.

How many emus and how many zebras are there?

Use algebra to help you work out the answer to this problem. Show all your workings.

There are 24 heads, so I started by writing $1e + 23z = 24$ … but 1 emu and 23 zebras have 94 legs in total, so that is not right!

Next I will try $5e + 19z$.

Stretch zone

Is there more than one possible answer? Justify your answer.

■ For more practice, go to Practice Book 6, page 93.

5D Problems with two unknowns

For more practice, go to Practice Book 6, page 94.

Explore

Key words
- unknown
- variable

More than one possibility

1 I am thinking of two positive integers that add up to 20.

What could the two numbers be?

I know there is more than one possible answer, but how many correct answers are there in total?

2 I am thinking of two positive numbers. Each number has one decimal place. The two numbers add up to 1.

What could the two numbers be?

3 I am thinking of two positive numbers. Each number has one decimal place. The two numbers add up to 2.

What could the two numbers be?

4 I am thinking of two positive numbers. Each number has two decimal places. The two numbers add up to 1.

Write down ten possible number pairs.

Can you explain your strategy?

Stretch zone

Think of a pair of numbers, both with two decimal places, that add up to 2. How many possible pairs of numbers do you think there are? Explain how you know you are correct.

■ For more practice, go to Practice Book 6, page 94.

5E Variables

Discover

Taxi fare variables

A taxi company calculates the taxi fare for each journey using the prices shown in the table below. There are some prices that remain constant and some prices that change for each taxi journey. The price that changes is called the variable.

Key words
- unknown
- variable
- constant
- equation

Small car	50¢ per kilometre	+ $1.50 per journey
Large car	70¢ per kilometre	+ $2.50 per journey
Luxury car	90¢ per kilometre	+ $3.50 per journey

What is the total fare for each of these taxi journeys?

1 4 km in a small car

2 7 km in a large car

3 8 km in a luxury car

4 16 km in a small car

5 28 km in a large car

6 32 km in a luxury car

7 84 km in a small car

8 105 km in a large car

> For a small car, the price of $1.50 per journey is constant. It is the same for every journey,
>
> The price per kilometre changes depending on the length of the journey. This is the variable.

Stretch zone

Write algebraic equations to calculate the taxi fare for the three types of car.

■ For more practice, go to Practice Book 6, page 95.

5E Variables

Explore

Write equations with variables

Play this game with a partner.

- Make a set of cards like these.

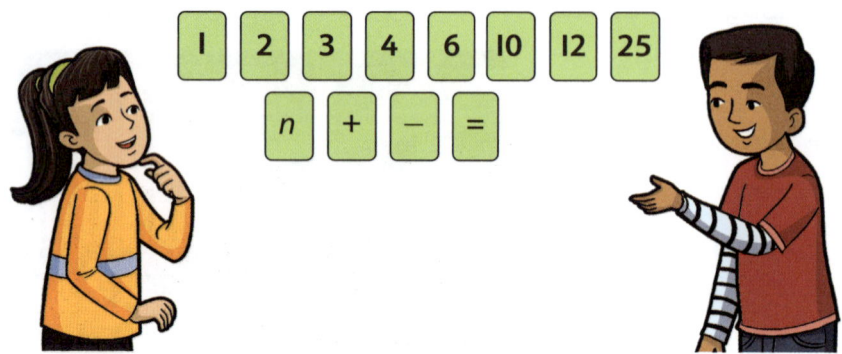

The letter n stands for an unknown number. This can be a different number each time.

- Use some of the cards to make an equation for a partner to solve.
- Your partner needs to find the value of n each time.

Repeat the game six times. Write the equations and the solutions in this table.

I made $2n + 6 = 12$. This means that $n = 3$. My partner answered correctly.

	Equation	Solution
	$2n + 6 = 12$	$n = 3$
1		
2		
3		
4		
5		
6		

Stretch zone

Add brackets to each of the equations in the table to change the value of n.

For example: $2(n + 6) = 12$, so $n = 0$.

108

5 Algebra

Connect

Investigate formulae

You are going to find out if there is a relationship between a person's height (h) and the circumference (c) of their head.

 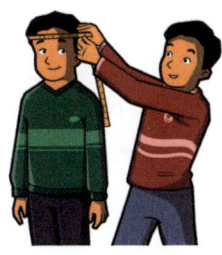

I Investigate this relationship. Complete this table for 10 students in your class.

Height (h)	Circumference of head (c)	$h \div c$

Everyone in your class will have a different circumference of their head and a different height.

Use a calculator to calculate $h \div c$. Round the answer to I decimal place when you write it in the table.

2 Look at the results in the table. Is there a relationship between the two measurements? Describe what you found out.

_____

_____

_____

 **Stretch zone**

Can you write a formula for finding a person's height (h), if we know the circumference of their head (c)?

Review

1 The numbers in each sequence increase or decrease by the same amount each time. Write the missing numbers.

a [ ] 55 61 [ ] [ ]

b [ ] 4 [ ] [ ] ⁻11

2 I have $25. I give some of my money (m) to charity. Which equation can I use to calculate how much money I have left (l)?

Circle the correct answer.

$l = 25 + m$ $l = 25 - m$ $l = 25 \times m$ $l = m - 25$ $l = m \div 25$

3 $a + 3b = 25$ a and b are whole numbers less than 20.

Write down three possible number pairs for a and b.

$a =$ [ ] $b =$ [ ] $a =$ [ ] $b =$ [ ] $a =$ [ ] $b =$ [ ]

4 Find the value of each pattern of shapes.

a  [ ]

b  [ ]

c   [ ]

● = 4

■ = 5

▲ = 6

d Use these shapes to draw a pattern with the value 27.

[   ]

5 The price of a personalised football shirt is $25 plus an additional $1.50 for each letter in the name.

$p = 25 + 1.5n$

In this formula p stands for price; n stands for the number of letters in the name.

Calculate the price of a football shirt with each of these names.

a Somchai $ [ ]   **b** Luis $ [ ]   **c** Ayesha $ [ ]

6 Length, mass and capacity

In this unit you will:

- use different units of measure, with up to three decimal places
- convert between different units of measure, with up to three decimal places
- convert between miles and kilometres
- solve measurement problems, including converting between units.

? Why do we need to convert between units?

Engage

Most people use measurements at work.

When can we use non-standard measures?

When do we not need to measure accurately?

Did you measure anything yesterday?

6A Comparing units of measure

Discover

Metric measurements

Draw a line to connect each item on the left to the correct measurement on the right.

Key words
- kilometre (km)
- tonne (t)
- standard units

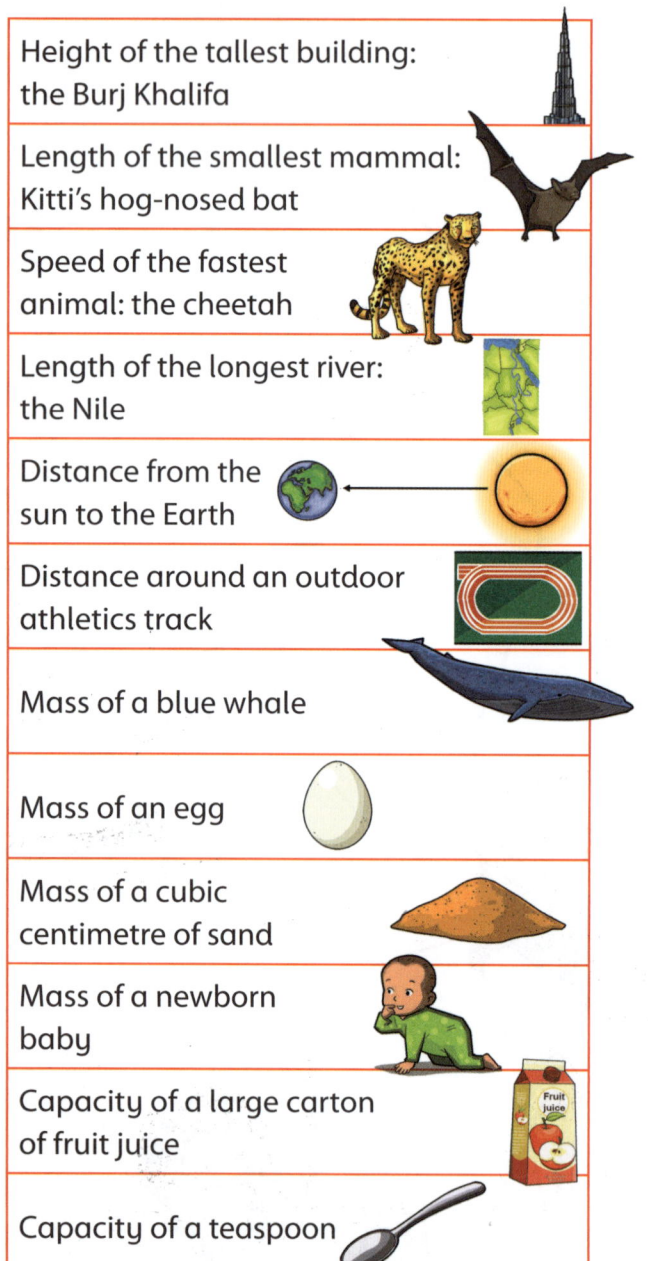

Height of the tallest building: the Burj Khalifa
Length of the smallest mammal: Kitti's hog-nosed bat
Speed of the fastest animal: the cheetah
Length of the longest river: the Nile
Distance from the sun to the Earth
Distance around an outdoor athletics track
Mass of a blue whale
Mass of an egg
Mass of a cubic centimetre of sand
Mass of a newborn baby
Capacity of a large carton of fruit juice
Capacity of a teaspoon

65 km per hour
6650 km
149 600 000 km
830 m
3.4 kg
3 cm
5 ml
1 litre
53 g
190 tonnes
2.6 g
400 m

1 tonne (t) = 1000 kg

Stretch zone

Use the internet to research the mass of other objects and animals that you would measure in tonnes.

For more practice, go to Practice Book 6, page 98.

6A Comparing units of measure

Explore

Equivalent measurements

1 Choose five pairs of facts from page 112. Write a sentence comparing each pair of facts.

from page 112

Key words
- kilometre (km)
- tonne (t)
- standard units

Worked example

'The height of the Burj Khalifa is about the same distance as two laps around an athletics track.'

a _____

_____

b _____

_____

For example: How many teaspoons are the equivalent of a carton of fruit juice? How many times greater than the mass of a baby is the mass of a blue whale?

I worked out that a baby weighs about the same as 1300 cubic centimetres of sand.

c _____

_____

d _____

_____

e _____

_____

6A Comparing units of measure

Explore (continued)

2 Colour all the boxes with equivalent measurements the same colour.

3 Write a new set of equivalent measurements in the empty boxes.

> There are seven sets of equivalent measurements. One has been done for you, so you will need six different colours.

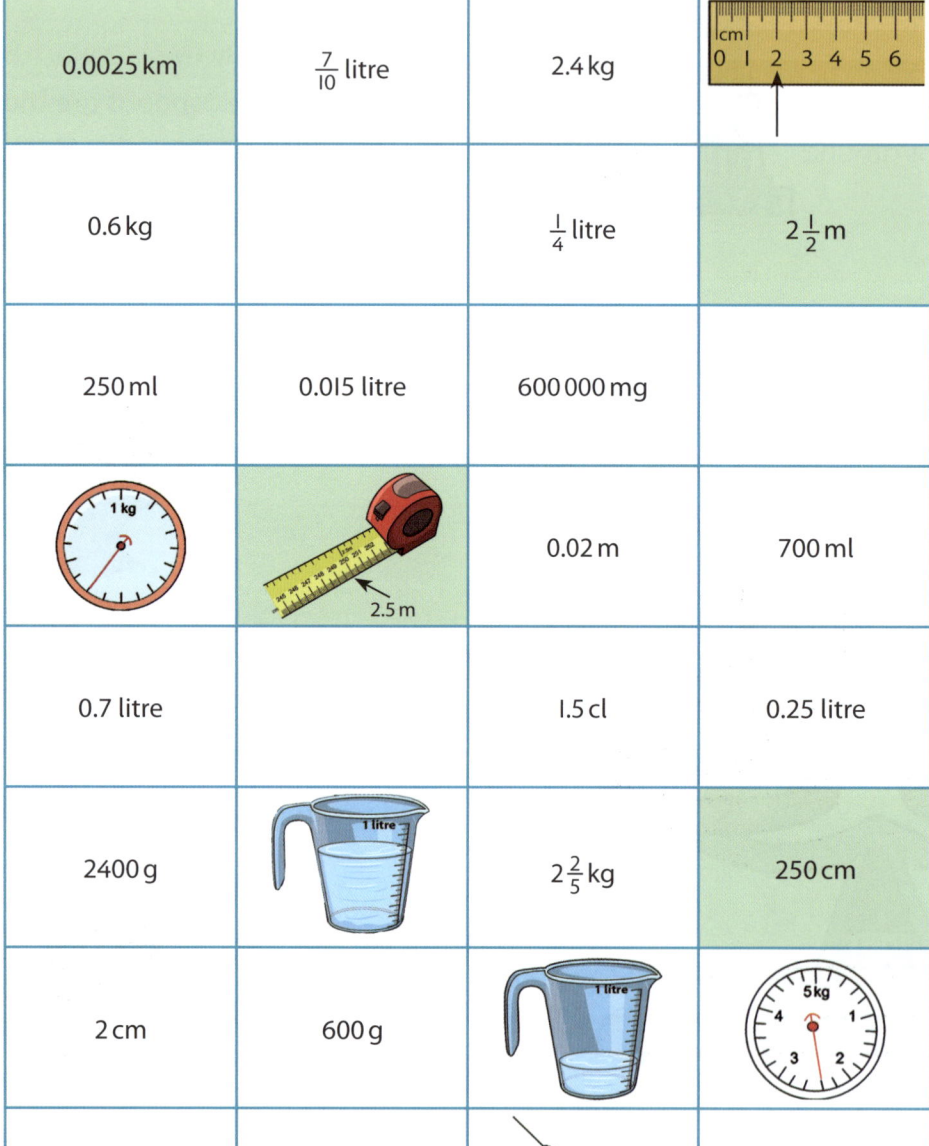

> Can you work out what units cl and mg stand for? Use your knowledge of other units of measure to help you work it out.

The grid contains:

0.0025 km	$\frac{7}{10}$ litre	2.4 kg	(ruler: cm 0 1 2 3 4 5 6, arrow at 2)
0.6 kg		$\frac{1}{4}$ litre	$2\frac{1}{2}$ m
250 ml	0.015 litre	600 000 mg	
(dial: 1 kg)	(tape measure: 2.5 m)	0.02 m	700 ml
0.7 litre		1.5 cl	0.25 litre
2400 g	(jug: 1 litre)	$2\frac{2}{5}$ kg	250 cm
2 cm	600 g	(jug: 1 litre)	(dial: 5 kg)
$\frac{15}{1000}$ litre		(syringe: 15 ml)	20 mm

Stretch zone

Make a poster of remarkable measurement facts for your classroom wall or a hallway in your school. Use the internet or books to research the facts.

114

■ For more practice, go to Practice Book 6, page 99.

6B Converting units of measure

Discover

Metric conversions

Think back

> There are 100 cm in 1 m. There are 10 mm in 1 cm.
>
> To convert centimetres to millimetres, we multiply by 10.
>
> To convert metres to centimetres, we multiply by 100.
>
> To convert metres to millimetres, we muliply by 1000.

Work with a partner.

1 Convert the units of measure and complete the first three columns of each table.

2 In the 'Object' column, write the name of an object for each measurement.

- For example, my teacher's chair is approximately 50.7 cm wide.

50.7 cm

Find objects with approximately these measurements. They do not have to be the exact measurements.

Length

Metres	Centimetres	Millimetres	Object
		1 mm	
		10 mm	
		34.5 mm	
	18 cm		
	50.7 cm		width of my teacher's chair
0.855 m			
10.3 m			
150 m			

Discover (continued)

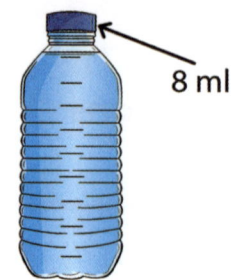

8 ml

> There are 100 cl in 1 litre. There are 10 ml in 1 cl.
>
> There are 1000 g in 1 kg. There are 1000 mg in 1 g.

Capacity

Litres	Centilitres	Millilitres	Object
		8 ml	*a bottle top*
		57 ml	
	25.9 cl		
	68.7 cl		
15.2 litres			
50 litres			

Mass

Kilograms	Grams	Milligrams	Object
		220 mg	
		675 mg	
	58 g		
	850 g		
22.5 kg			
175 kg			

Stretch zone

Can you write some rules for converting between different units?

■ For more practice, go to Practice Book 6, page 100.

6B Converting units of measure

Explore

Metric word problems

Key words
- convert units
- milli-
- centi-
- kilo-

1 The average width of one currant is approximately 3 mm.

Calculate how many currants you can fit into the length of:

a your desk

b your classroom.

Use your answer to **question 1a** to help you answer **question 1b**.

2 The mass of 300 uncooked lentils is approximately 5 g.

The mass of an average adult man in Brazil is 72 kg. What is his mass in lentils?

3 A can of fizzy drink has a capacity of 25 centilitres.

A small bucket holds approximately 4.5 litres.

How many cans of drink will fill the bucket?

Explore (continued)

4 Think about the coins you use in your country.

a Which coin has the highest value?

b How much does that coin weigh?  g

c The mass of a gold bullion bar is 12.4 kg.

How many of the coins from **question 4a** weigh the same as the gold bullion bar?

d What is the total value of these coins?

5 a What is the distance between your home and your school, in kilometres? km

b Measure the length of your stride.

My stride is m.

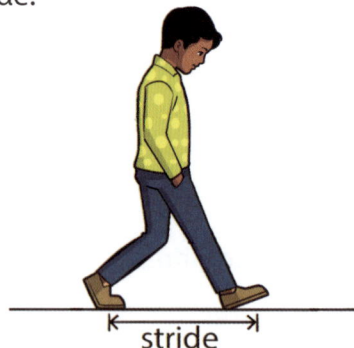

stride

> Your stride is the distance you move forwards in one step.

c How many strides do you need to take to walk from your home to your school?

Stretch zone

Compare the length of your stride with someone else's stride. What is the difference between the number of strides you both need to take to walk from your home to your school?

■ For more practice, go to Practice Book 6, page 101.

6C Reading scales and measuring accurately

Discover

Key words
- scale drawing
- trundle wheel

Measure and use scales to draw a map

Work in a small group.

You are going to make a scale drawing of your school and grounds.

- Use a trundle wheel to measure longer distances and a metre stick or tape measure to measure shorter distances.

- Use squared paper for your drawing.

You will need to find a map of your school. You could use a map from the internet.

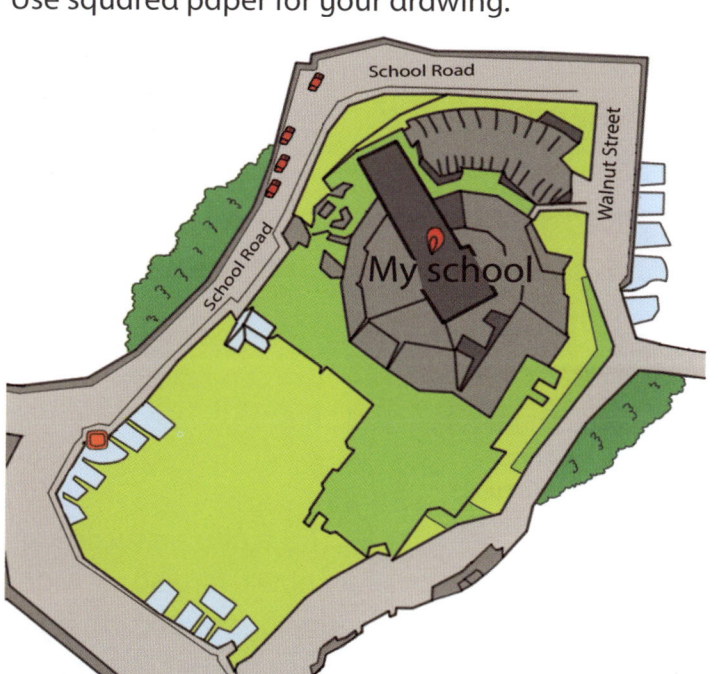

If I use a scale of 1 cm to 1 m, will my map fit on the paper?

1 First decide what measurements you need to take.

- Decide which features you will include.

- Decide what scale you are going to use.

2 Make a draft version of your scale drawing.

- Share the draft with another group to get their feedback.

3 Use their feedback when you make your final drawing.

What about a scale of 0.5 cm to 1 m?

Stretch zone

Present your finished scale drawing to an adult. Explain all the features to them and how you measured everything so that your drawing was to scale.

6 Length, mass and capacity

119

■ For more practice, go to Practice Book 6, page 102.

Explore

Reading scales

1 Mark the rulers to show these lengths.

a 4.5 cm

b 0.5 cm

c 11.5 cm

d 15.5 cm

e 23.5 cm

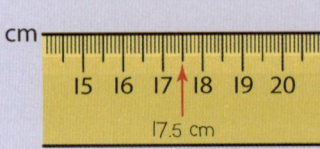

I have marked this ruler to show 17.5 cm

2 Mark the measuring jugs, to a reasonable degree of accuracy, to show these volumes.

a 170 ml

c 35 ml

b 890 ml

d 460 ml

The scales on these jugs show every 50 ml. Mark the jugs as accurately as you can, but your marks do not have to be exact.

6C Reading scales and measuring accurately

Explore (continued)

3 Draw the pointers on the scales to show these masses.

a 950 g

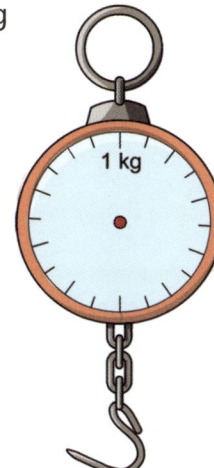

c 520 g

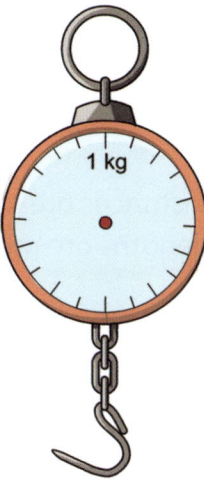

> I have marked this scale to show 825 g.
>
> 825 g

b 15 g

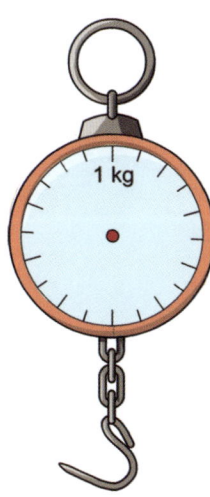

d 430 g

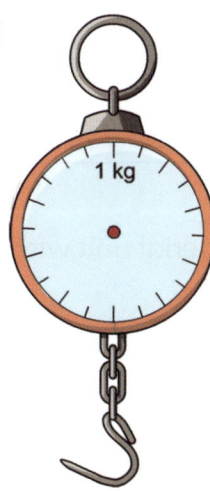

4 Draw lines with these lengths.

a 10.7 cm

b 5.3 cm

c 1.2 cm

> Draw your lines accurate to the nearest millimetre.

Stretch zone

Look at some scales that use inches and feet (length), ounces and pounds (mass) or fluid ounces (capacity and volume). Compare these imperial scales with metric scales. What is the same and what is different?

■ For more practice, go to Practice Book 6, page 103.

6D Imperial units

Discover

Investigate imperial units

Sometimes we use different units, called imperial units.

Worked example

Miles

In some countries, including the USA, distances are measured in miles instead of kilometres. Smaller lengths are measured in feet instead of metres.

NEXT SERVICES
57 MILES

Miles ___A kilometre is approximately $\frac{5}{8}$ of a mile.___

Use the internet or an encyclopedia to find out about different units.

1 Write a sentence comparing each imperial unit with an appropriate metric unit.

   a Feet _____

   b Inches _____

   c Pounds _____

   d Ounces _____

   e Pints _____

2 In a group, research some interesting facts about an animal.

Prepare a presentation. Include the following facts about the animal. You must use imperial units.

- The mass of the animal
- The length of the animal
- How fast the animal can run, swim or fly

You can choose any animal you like.

Stretch zone

Convert all the measurements from your presentation into metric units.

122

6D Imperial units

Explore

Miles and kilometres

Key words
- imperial units
- metric units
- mile
- kilometre
- conversion graph

Think back

5 miles is approximately equal to 8 km.

1 Complete this table to help you convert from kilometres to miles.

Miles	1	2	5	10	15	20	50	100
Kilometres			8					

You will need to decide on the scale for your graph.

2 Use this information to draw a conversion graph below.

Stretch zone

Look at the photo at the top of this page. Can you convert all these distances into miles? What calculation did you use for each one?

123

■ For more practice, go to Practice Book 6, page 105.

6 Length, mass and capacity

We can convert between units to solve everyday problems with different metric units and we can convert between metric and imperial units.

Connect

Pastry problem

Imagine you work at a company that makes pies.

The pastry-rolling machine rolls out rectangles of pastry that measure 1 m by 75 cm.

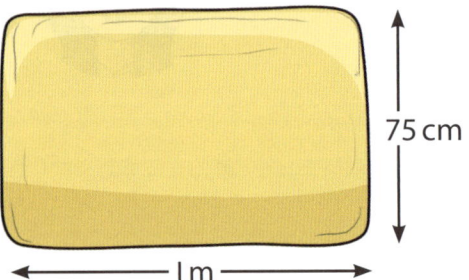

75 cm

1 m

The circular base of each pie has a diameter of 8 cm. The circular top of each pie has a diameter of 4 cm.

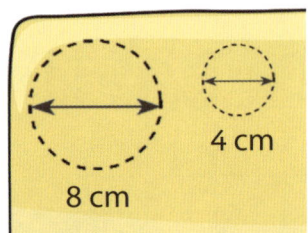

4 cm

8 cm

How can you cut one rectangle of pastry to make the maximum number of pies?

 Work in a group. On a large piece of paper draw, a diagram to show your solution.

Make sure that you draw the same number of pie bases as pie tops.

Stretch zone

Each pie contains 25 ml of filling. The company buys the filling in 250 ml jars. How much filling do you need to fill all the pies you make? How many jars of filling do you need?

6 Length, mass and capacity

Review

1 Look at this measuring jug.

    a How much water is there in the jug?  ml

    b How much water do I need to add so there is I litre in the jug?  ml

2 What is $\frac{3}{4}$ kg in grams? [____] g

3 I walk 350 m in 5 minutes. How far do I walk in I hour? [____] km

4 Write these measurements in order. Start with the shortest.

| 1.25 km | 0.95 km | 1500 m | 750 m | 1000 cm |

[____] [____] [____] [____] [____]

5 Draw a line that is exactly 5.9 cm long.

6 This table shows the height of three mountains, in metres.

Mountain	Height in m
Everest	8848
Kilimanjaro	5895
Kinabalu	4095

    a How much higher is Mount Everest than Mount Kilimanjaro? [____] m

    b A mountaineer climbs Mount Kilimanjaro and Mount Kinabalu. How many more metres has she climbed than the height of Mount Everest?  m

7 On a scale drawing, I cm represents 0.25 m.

On the drawing, a table is 2 cm wide and 5 cm long. What are the dimensions of the real table, in centimetres?

[____] cm wide   [____] cm long

In this unit you will:

- recognise that shapes with the same area can have different perimeters and vice versa
- recognise when it is possible to use formulae to calculate the area and volume of shapes
- calculate the area of parallelograms and triangles
- calculate, estimate and compare the volume of cubes and cuboids.

?

How can I find perimeters, areas and volumes of more complex shapes?

Engage

Does every shape with an area of 16 cm² have the same perimeter?

Does every shape with a perimeter of 24 cm have the same area?

I don't think that is always true.

There are lots of different shapes with the same area.

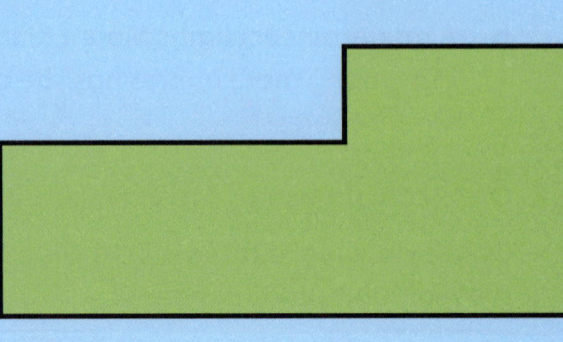

If I double the perimeter of a shape, will the new area be double the original area?

7A Area and perimeter of rectilinear shapes

Discover

Different shapes with the same perimeter

Think back

A rectilinear shape has straight sides that all meet at right angles. To calculate the area of a rectilinear shape, divide the shape into rectangles and work out the area of each rectangle.

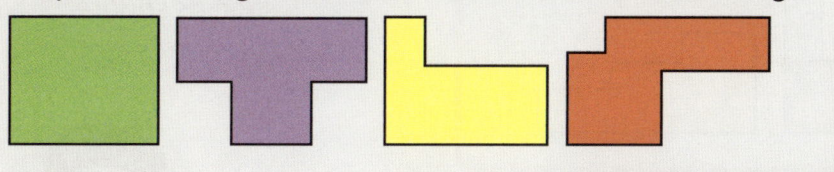

Key words
- area
- perimeter
- rectilinear shape

We can calculate the area of a rectangle using the formula:

Area = length × width

A farmer has 24 metres of wire fencing.

He wants to enclose the largest possible area of land to allow his goats to graze.

What shape of enclosure should he choose? Draw some of the possible rectangles and other rectilinear shapes.

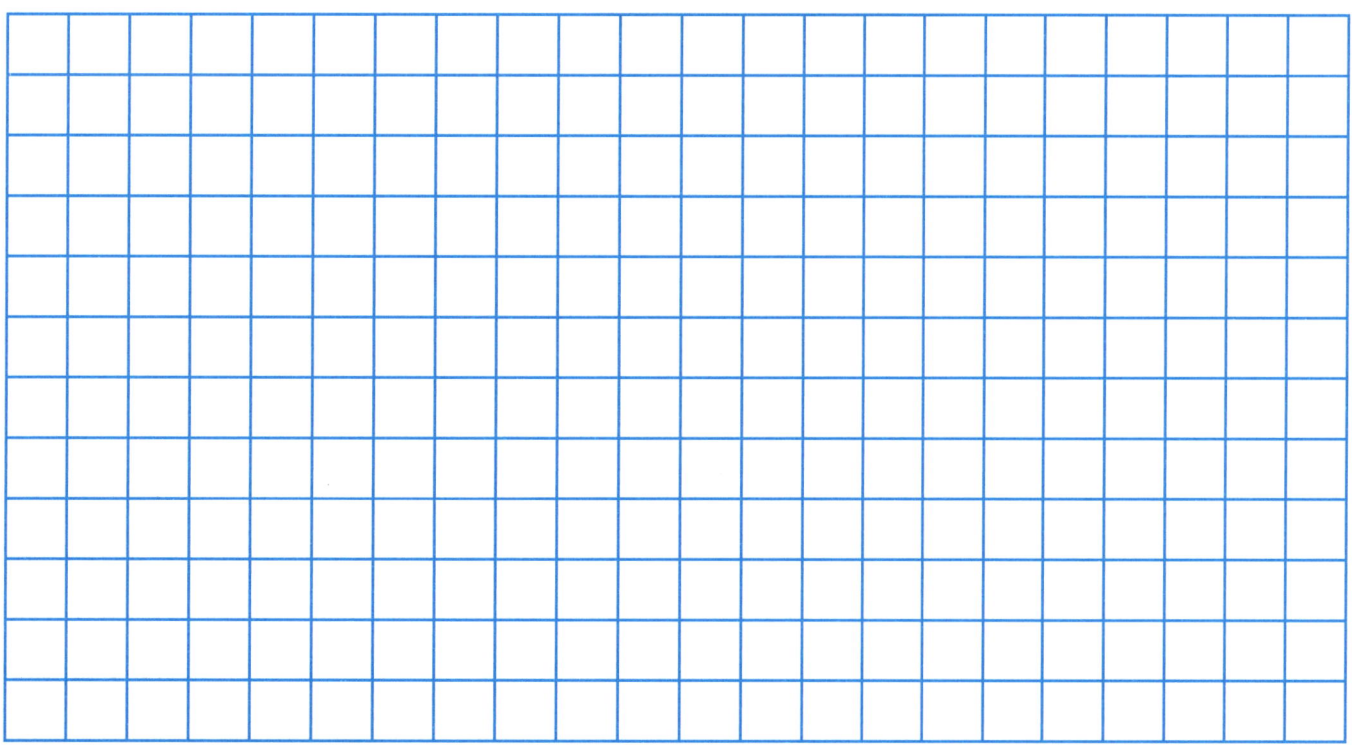

Stretch zone

Explore this problem using other polygons, such as a regular hexagon or octagon.

■ For more practice, go to Practice Book 6, page 107.

7A Area and perimeter of rectilinear shapes

Explore

Different shapes with the same area

Think back

Rectilinear shapes are not just rectangles. A rectilinear shape can have any number of sides that all meet at right angles.

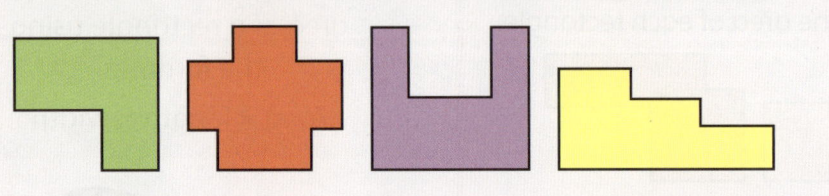

Remember, we measure area in square units such as square centimetres (cm²).

I Draw two different rectilinear shapes with an area of 36 cm² on this centimetre-squared grid.

- Write the perimeter under each shape.

2 On centimetre-squared paper, draw four rectilinear shapes with an area of 68 cm² and four with an area of 125 cm².

Stretch zone

Draw four different quadrilaterals, each with an area of 36 cm².

■ For more practice, go to Practice Book 6, page 108.

7B Finding the area of triangles and parallelograms

Discover

Key words
- length
- perpendicular height
- formula

Area of a triangle and a parallelogram

1 Draw three different rectangles on this centimetre-squared grid.

- Find the area of each rectangle. Write the area under the rectangle.

2 Divide each rectangle into two triangles by drawing a diagonal line between two opposite vertices.

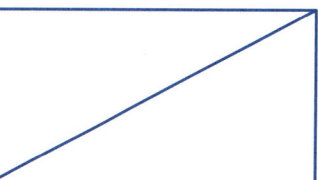

3 Find the area of each triangle by counting the squares.

- Write the area under each triangle.

4 Compare the area of each rectangle and each triangle.

- What do you notice?

_____

_____

Discover (continued)

5 Draw three parallelograms on this centimetre-squared grid.

- Find the area of each parallelogram by counting the squares.
- Write the area under each parallelogram.

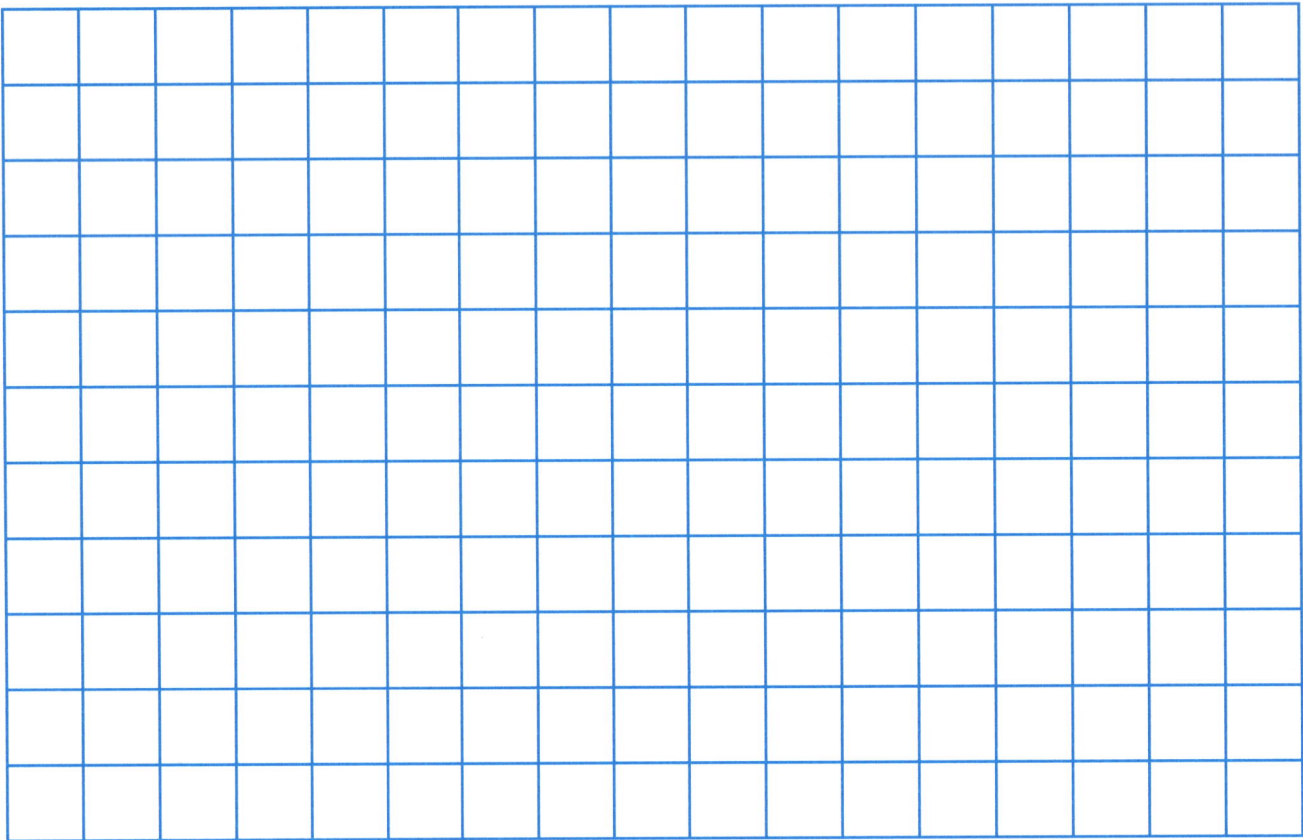

6 Copy your parallelograms onto squared paper and cut them out.

- Now make a rectangle by moving a triangle from one end to the other, as shown in this diagram.

7 Compare the area of each parallelogram and each rectangle. What do you notice?

_____

_____

Stretch zone

Use what you have learned in this lesson to write the formula for the area of any triangle and the formula for the area of any parallelogram. Explain to a partner why these formulae always work.

■ For more practice, go to Practice Book 6, page 109.

7B Finding the area of triangles and parallelograms

Explore

Key words
- perpendicular height
- formula

Draw triangles and parallelograms

Think back

These are the formulae for finding the areas of triangles and parallelograms:

Triangle: Area = $\frac{1}{2}$ (base × perpendicular height)

Parallelogram: Area = base × perpendicular height

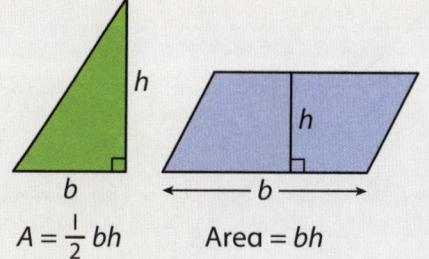

$A = \frac{1}{2} bh$ Area = bh

Use the formulae above to help you draw three different triangles, each with an area of 12 cm², and three different parallelograms, each with an area of 24 cm².

Stretch zone

Compare your three triangles. What is the same and what is different?

Compare your three parallelograms. What is the same and what is different?

■ For more practice, go to Practice Book 6, page 110.

Discover

Key words
- tangram
- dimension
- area
- formula

Tangram areas

Write the area of each shape in the tangram.

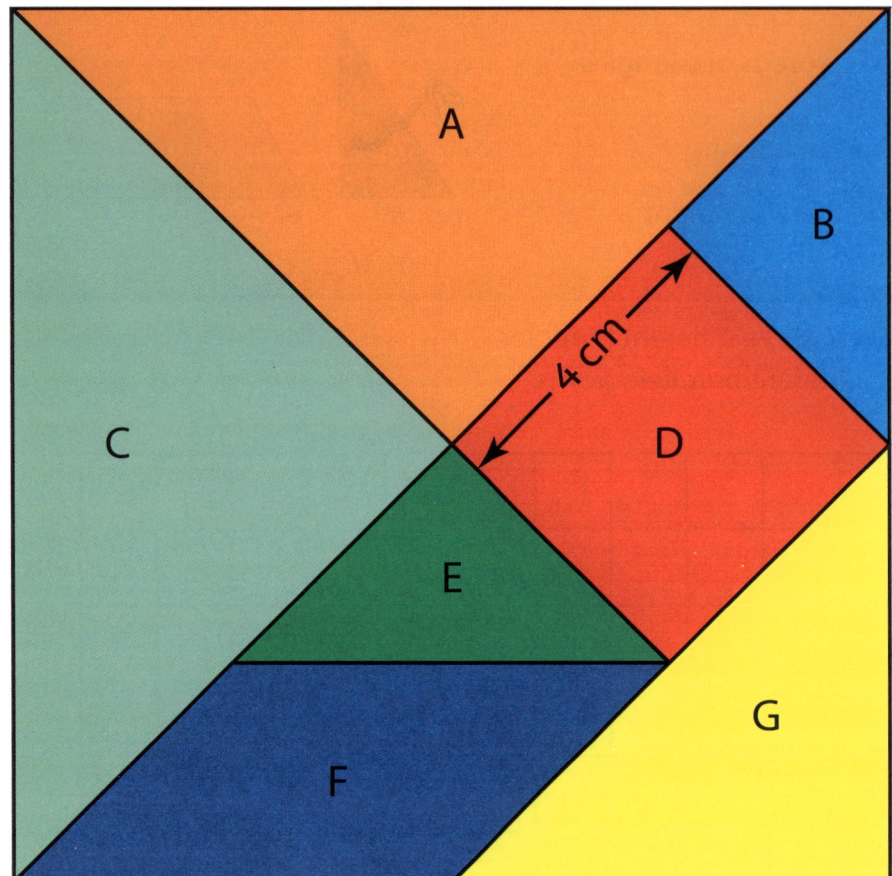

Use a formula to work out each area.

Which shape will you start with?

The areas of the shapes:

A ☐ cm²   E ☐ cm²

B ☐ cm²   F ☐ cm²

C ☐ cm²   G ☐ cm²

D ☐ cm²

Stretch zone

Compare shapes with the same area. Do they all have the same perimeter?
How will you work out the perimeters?

■ For more practice, go to Practice Book 6, page 111.

Explore

Explore different areas

1 Use the tangram pieces from page 132 to make new shapes.

- Calculate the total area of each shape that you make.
- Sketch all your shapes.

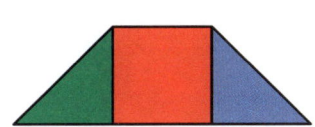 

Key words
- area
- formula
- composite shape

a Two different shapes using three pieces.

I made these shapes using three pieces. My shapes have areas of 32 cm² and 40 cm².

b Two different shapes using four pieces.

c Two different shapes using five pieces.

Remember: a sketch is a rough drawing. It does not need to be drawn accurately or to scale.

d Two different shapes using six pieces.

e Two different shapes using all seven pieces.

2 Compare the areas of your two shapes in each question.

- What do you notice about the areas of your shapes in **question 1e**? Can you explain why this happens?

_____

_____

Stretch zone

Use the tangram pieces to make parallelograms with these areas:

- 32 cm²
- 48 cm²
- 64 cm².

■ For more practice, go to Practice Book 6, page 112.

7D Calculating volume

Discover

Compare volumes

Think back

The formula for the volume of a cuboid is:

Volume = length × width × height

Key words
- volume
- length
- width
- height

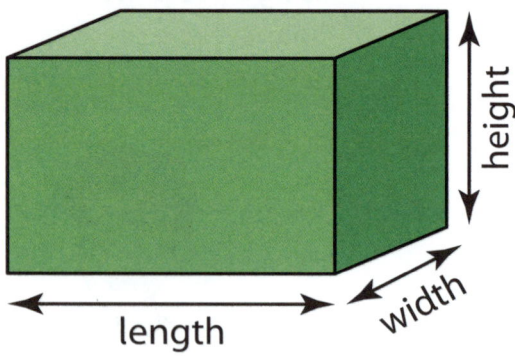

I Use two pieces of A4 paper to make two different open cuboids.

- Fold one piece of paper horizontally.
- Fold the other piece of paper vertically.

2 Work in a group.

- Investigate whether the two cuboids have the same volume or different volumes.

3 Write about what you found out.

_____

_____

_____

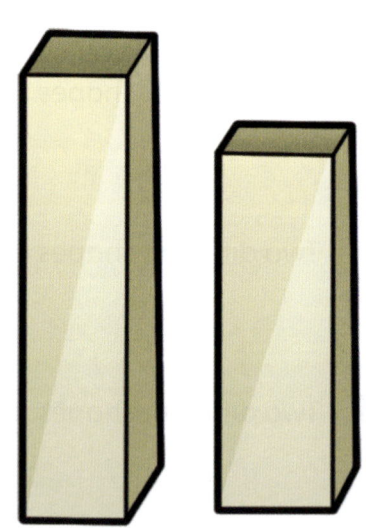

 4 Now use a piece of A3 paper and repeat the investigation. What do you notice?

_____

_____

 **Stretch zone**

Do you think the result will be the same for any size of paper? Try it out!

■ For more practice, go to Practice Book 6, page 113.

7D Calculating volume

Explore

Swimming pool dimensions

This is a sketch of a swimming pool that measures 12 m × 5 m.

The concrete surround is 1 m wide all the way around, and 20 cm high.

Answer the questions below. Show all your workings.

Key words
- area
- volume

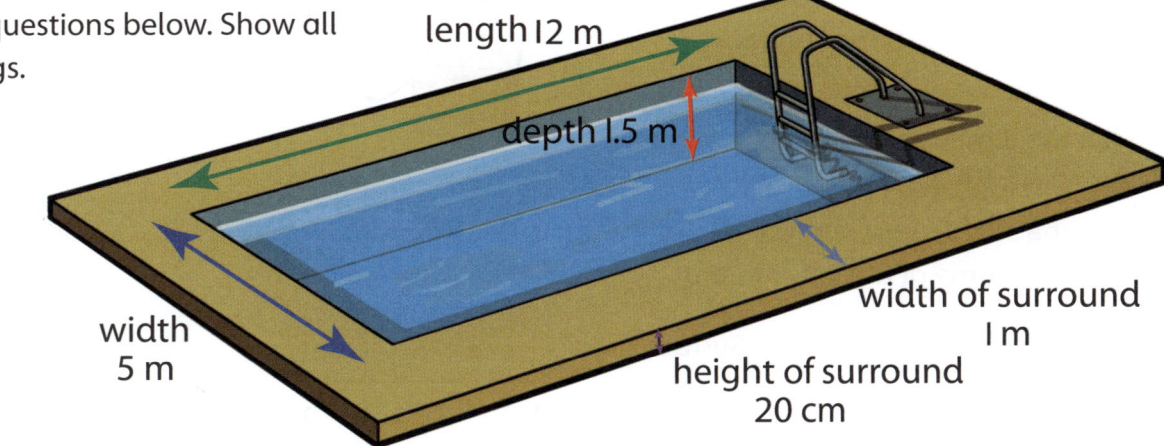

length 12 m

depth 1.5 m

width 5 m

width of surround 1 m

height of surround 20 cm

1 How much concrete is needed for the surround? Give your answer in cubic centimetres.

2 The concrete surround is covered in tiles. What area of tiling is needed to cover the surround? Give your answer in square metres.

3 The pool is 1.5 m deep. What volume of water is needed to fill the pool? Give your answer in litres.

1000 litres = 1 cubic metre

Stretch zone

Investigate the volume of water needed for different swimming pools with the same length and width but varying depths. You can even include a shallow end and a deep end.

135

■ For more practice, go to Practice Book 6, page 114.

7 Area, perimeter and volume

Connect

Stock cube boxes

Imagine that you work for a company that sells stock cubes.

The company sells the stock cubes in boxes of 12, 24 and 40.

Each stock cube is a 2 cm cube.

- Design each of the three boxes.
- Sketch the net of each box in your notebook.
- Write the dimensions of each box in the space below.
- Write the **surface area** (total area of the net), the perimeter and the volume of the finished box.

Use cubes to model each box.

1 Box of 12 cubes

Dimensions:

Surface area:

Perimeter:

Volume:

2 Box of 24 cubes

Dimensions:

Surface area:

Perimeter:

Volume:

3 Box of 40 cubes

Dimensions:

Surface area:

Perimeter:

Volume:

Compare your nets with a partner. What is the same? What is different?

Stretch zone

The company decides to sell the stock cubes in boxes of 100. Sketch the net of a box for 100 cubes that has the smallest possible surface area.

7 Area, perimeter and volume

Review

1 A square and a regular hexagon have the same perimeter.
  One side of the hexagon is 3 cm.

  a What is the perimeter of the square?

  b What is the area of the square?

2 I make this cuboid using centimetre cubes.

  a What is the volume of this cuboid?

  b I make a new cuboid. The length, width and height are
    all double the dimensions of the first cuboid. What is the
    volume of this new cuboid?

3 This is a net of a cuboid.

  a What is the volume of the cuboid?

  b What is the surface area of the cuboid?

Remember to include
the units in all your
answers. Do you need
cm, cm² or cm³?

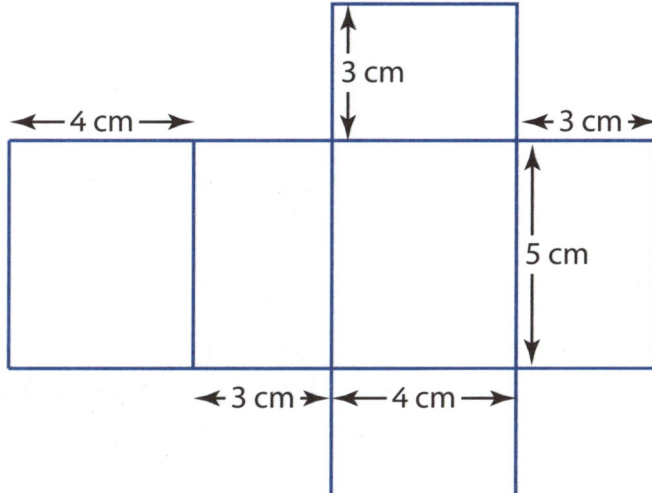

4 A square tile measures 25 cm by 25 cm. A rectangular tile is
  5 cm longer and 5 cm narrower.

  a What is the difference between
    the areas of the two tiles?

  b What is the total area of both tiles?

In this unit you will:

- solve problems that involve converting between units of time.

Engage

Is it possible for a person to live for a million hours?

How many different clocks, watches or timers do you see in a typical day?

?

How can I convert between units of time to solve problems and calculate time intervals?

How many hours do I spend in school in one year?

How do timetables help us know where we need to be?

How many minutes have there been so far this year?

I sleep for 8 hours each night. How many hours will I sleep during my whole life?

Discover

Times with consecutive digits

On a digital 24-hour clock, at certain times all the digits except the zeros are consecutive.

Key words
- digital clock
- analogue clock
- consecutive
- 12-hour clock
- 24-hour clock

These are the same times on analogue clocks.

Quarter to 4    Six minutes to 7

Find out how many times with consecutive digits there are in each time interval.

- The times must contain no more than one zero.

1 between 23:00 and 05:00

Record your answers as analogue times and as digital times.

2 between 09:00 and 13:00

You can choose to write the times or draw the clocks.

 Stretch zone

Predict the number of times there are with consecutive digits between midday and midnight. Then investigate. Explain how you know you have found all the times.

■ For more practice, go to Practice Book 6, page 116.

Explore

Problems with units of time

Key words
- millennium
- century
- decade
- millisecond

Think back

There are 100 years in a century and 1000 years in a millennium.

1 Complete this table. Two are done for you

Number of centuries in a millennium	
Number of decades in a century	
Number of years in a decade	10
Number of months in a year	
Number of weeks in a year	

Number of days in a week	7
Number of hours in a day	
Number of minutes in an hour	
Number of seconds in a minute	
Number of milliseconds in a second	

Use the information in the table to answer these questions.

- Show all your workings.

2 How many hours have there been in this year so far?

[   ] hours

Remember leap years and use the correct number of days in each month in your calculation!

3 How many days old are you?

[   ] days

I am 11 years, 4 months and 12 days old. I am 4151 days old!

4 Find someone in your school or at home who is younger than you. How many days younger than you are they?

[   ] days

8A Converting between units of time

Explore (continued)

5 How many milliseconds are there in a maths lesson?

| | milliseconds

There are 1000 milliseconds in a second.

6 Choose two different historical events. How many decades ago did they happen?

a _____ | | decades ago

b _____ | | decades ago

7 It takes the planet Saturn approximately 29.5 Earth years to orbit the sun.

a How many months is this? | |

b How many days is this? | |

8 A famous fast food restaurant sells approximately 375 burgers every 5 seconds. Approximately how many burgers do they sell

a in one hour? | |

b in one day? | |

You can use a calculator to help you with these questions!

Stretch zone

What date is 1 million days after the start of this millennium?

■ For more practice, go to Practice Book 6, page 117.

8B Using the 24-hour clock and timetables

Discover

Key words
- 24-hour clock
- timetable

Different timetables

Think back

The time on a 24-hour clock always has four digits.
For example, 6:35 a.m. is 06:35 on a 24-hour clock.

Worked example

Here is a timetable for a day at the zoo.

09:00	10:15–11:00	11:00–12:30	12:30–13:45	13:45–14:30	14:30–15:20	15:20–16:00	16:00
Leave home	Arrive, have a snack in the cafe	The reptile house	Lunch and adventure playground	The primates	The big cats	The big five safari	Go home

Complete these timetables with activities of your choice.

1 A school day

2 A day on holiday

Stretch zone

Write a two-part word problem based on one of your timetables. Give your problem to a partner to solve.

■ For more practice, go to Practice Book 6, page 118.

Explore

Design a bus timetable

You are going to design a route for buses in your town.

The route must start at the bus station and stop at five different places in the town before returning to the bus station.

1 Draw a simple map to show the bus route. Include:

- the bus station and the five stops
- the time interval between each stop.

Key words

- 24-hour clock
- timetable

The first journey must start at 09:00 and the last journey must start at 19:30.

2 Complete the bus timetable. Include 10 different bus journeys for your route.

Bus station	09:00									19:30
Stop 1										
Stop 2										
Stop 3										
Stop 4										
Stop 5										
Bus station										

Stretch zone

Write a two-part word problem based on your bus timetable. Give your problem to a partner to solve.

8 Time

■ For more practice, go to Practice Book 6, page 119.

8C Time zone problems

Discover

World time zones

Look at this map of time zones around the world.

Key words
- time zone
- time difference

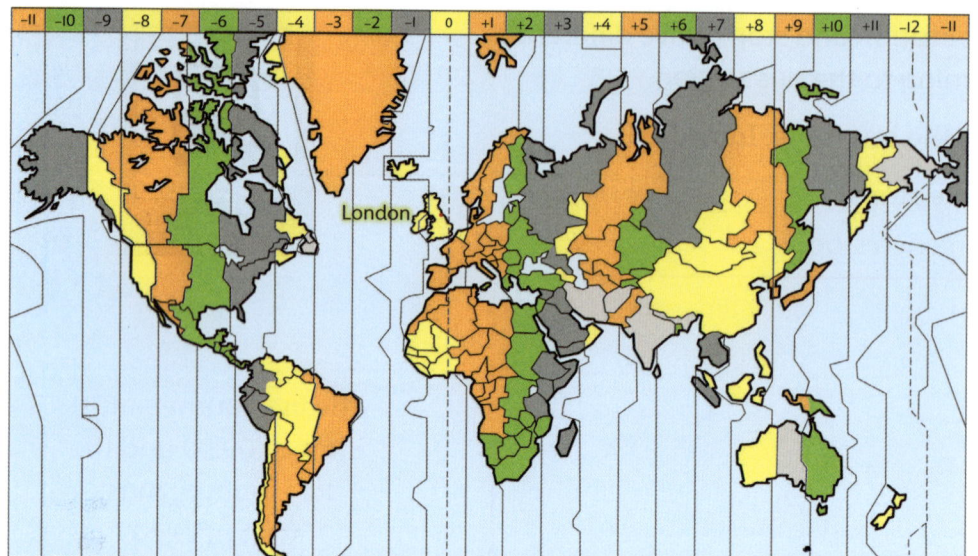

When it is 6 o'clock in the evening in Dubai, it is 2 o'clock in the afternoon in London.

Use this map to write six facts about times around the world.

1 _____

_____

2 _____

_____

3 _____

_____

4 _____

_____

5 _____

_____

6 _____

_____

Western Australia is 2 hours behind eastern Australia, so when it is 10 p.m. in Sydney, it is 8 p.m. in Perth.

Stretch zone

What is the time difference between London and where you live?
What is the time in London now? What is the time in Sydney, Australia?

■ For more practice, go to Practice Book 6, page 120.

8C Time zone problems

Explore

Time zone problems

Key words
- time zone
- time difference

Use a world map to find out where all these places are.

1   What is the best time to have a video call with someone in Australia?

2   Your cousin in California goes to bed at 22:20. What time is this where you live?

3   You come home from school at 16:00. What time is this in Belgium?

Show all your workings. Write your answers using 24-hour clock times.

4   Does someone in Argentina celebrate New Year before or after you? Circle the correct word.

Before / After

By how many hours?

5   You fly from New York to Tokyo. The flight takes 14 hours. It leaves New York at 09:30. What time do you arrive in Tokyo (local time)?

6   Your class is twinned with a class in Madagascar.

When is the best time to have a video call?

Explain your answer.

_____

Stretch zone

Think of a city that is in a different time zone. Research the flights from your country to this city. How long is the flight? If your flight is at 13:00, what will the local time be when you arrive?

■ For more practice, go to Practice Book 6, page 121.

8 Time

I can convert between units of time using multiplication or division. I can use time conversion facts and timetables to solve real-life time problems.

Connect

School day trip

You are planning a school day trip to an island.

These are the rules:

- You cannot be on the island when the tide is high.
- You cannot depart from school before 08:30.
- You must be back at school by 15:45.
- The journey to the coast takes 45 minutes.
- You want to spend at least 4 hours on the island.

There are four possible dates for the trip. This timetable shows the times when the tide is high.

5 July	08:00–10:00	15:00–17:00
12 July	10:00–12:00	17:00–19:00
19 July	12:00–14:00	19:00–21:00
26 July	14:00–16:00	21:00–23:00

1 How long can you spend on the island on each date?

5 July _____   19 July _____

12 July _____   26 July _____

2 Which is the best date for your school trip? Why?

_____

3 In your notebook, draw a timetable for the day trip.

Which is the worst day to visit the island?

Stretch zone

There are some new rules! Now you can change **either** the time you leave school **or** the amount of time on the island. Which will you change and why?

8 Time

Review

1 How many days are there in March, April and May altogether?  days

2 The Olympic Games are held every 4 years. The Olympic Games in 2020 were cancelled. In what year were the Olympic Games before 2020 held?

3 Eric, Olivia and Harriet go for a long walk. They start at 13:00. Eric takes 2 hours and 37 minutes.

   a Olivia takes 12 minutes longer than Eric. At what time does Olivia finish the walk?

   b Harriet takes 5 minutes less than Eric. At what time does she finish?

4 I go to school for 8 hours each day. For what fraction of a day am I at school?

5 Look at this timetable of trains from Bangkok to Chiang Mai.

Departs Bangkok	06:30	07:05	07:35	08:05	08:35	09:05
Arrives Chiang Mai	17:35	18:15	18:57	19:08	19:42	20:12

   a You need to arrive in Chiang Mai before 7 p.m. What is the departure time of the latest train you can catch?

   b At what time does the fastest train depart?

6 This is a timetable for Paulo's mornings at school this week.

Time	Monday	Tuesday	Wednesday	Thursday	Friday
08:30 – 10:00	Mathematics	English	Science	Mathematics	English
10:00 – 10:20	Break	Break	Break	Break	Break
10:20 – 12:00	Social Science	Mathematics	English	Science	History

What is the total number of minutes of Mathematics on this timetable? minutes

In this unit you will:

- draw 2D shapes using given dimensions and angles
- recognise, describe and build simple 3D shapes
- compare and classify geometric shapes
- illustrate and name parts of a circle
- recognise angles and find missing angles.

? How can I describe, draw and make 2D and 3D shapes?

Engage

I can see lots of different shapes.

What 3D shapes can you see? Can you name them?

What 2D shapes can you see? Can you name them?

Which shapes form tessellating patterns?

9A Classifying 2D shapes

Discover

Key words
- edge
- vertex/vertices
- polygon
- properties

Make 2D shapes

Think back

Here are some 2D shapes that you know. They are all quadrilaterals.

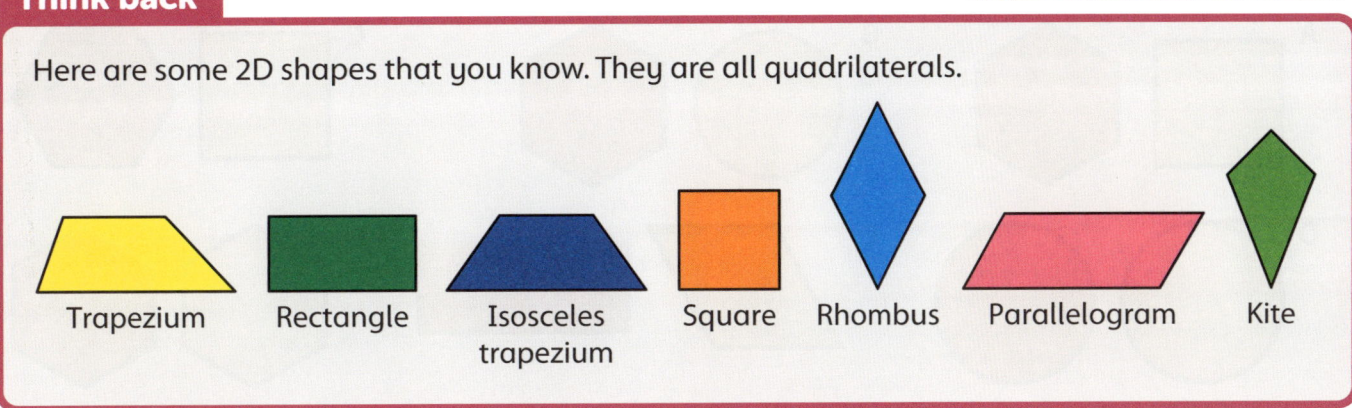

Trapezium   Rectangle   Isosceles trapezium   Square   Rhombus   Parallelogram   Kite

1 Look at these pairs of shapes.

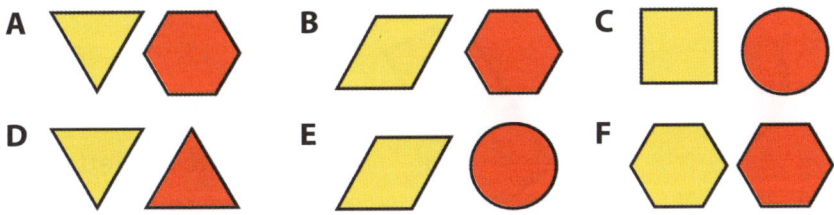

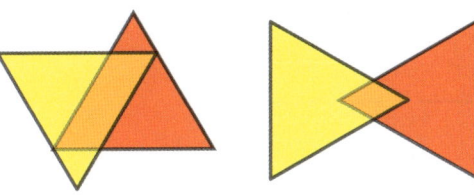

- Copy the shapes onto card and cut them out.
- Use one pair of shapes.
- Move one shape on top of the other shape. The overlapping parts will create new shapes.

2 What shapes can you make with each pair of overlapping shapes?

- Sketch some of your shapes.

I used the two equilateral triangles. I made a parallelogram and a rhombus.

Can you name any of the shapes you have made?

Discover (continued)

3 Repeat the activity with these pairs of shapes.

What shapes can you make by overlapping the pairs of shapes?

4 Circle the shapes that you can make.

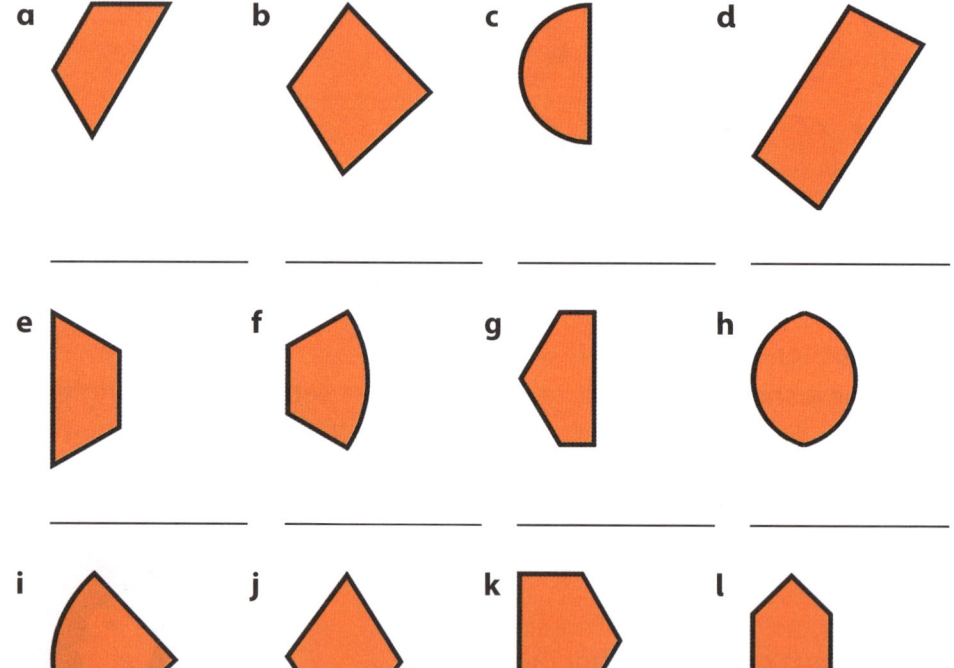

Write the letter of the pair of shapes from **question 3** next to each shape that you can make.

Write the name of the shape under each shape.

Stretch zone

Can you overlap shapes to make all the quadrilaterals in the 'Think back' box on page 149?

■ For more practice, go to Practice Book 6, page 123.

Explore

Draw 2D shapes

I Draw a different triangle in each section of this table and write its name.

	No right angles	One right angle
No sides equal		
Two sides equal		
Three sides equal		

Key words
- regular
- irregular
- parallel
- internal angle

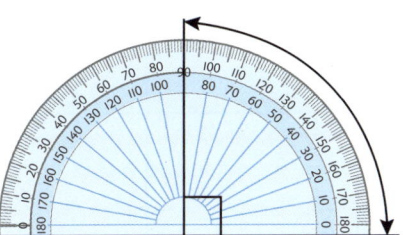

Use a protractor to draw the right angles.

2 Draw a different polygon in each section of this table.

	Regular	Irregular
Quadrilateral		
Pentagon		
Hexagon		

Can you explain why some sections of the table in **question I** might be empty?

Stretch zone

Write clear instructions for a partner to draw an irregular pentagon. Two sides should be 4.5 cm long and two angles should be 60°.

9 Geometry – properties of shapes

■ For more practice, go to Practice Book 6, page 124.

9B Properties of 2D shapes

Discover 1

Classify 2D shapes

Draw at least one polygon in each section of this table.

- Label each shape with its name.

Key words
- polygon
- regular
- irregular
- parallel

	No parallel sides	One pair of parallel sides	Two pairs of parallel sides
No equal sides			
One pair of equal sides			
Two pairs of equal sides			

Stretch zone

Draw any lines of symmetry in the polygons above.

■ For more practice, go to Practice Book 6, page 125.

Discover 2

Rotational symmetry in 2D shapes

Key words
- rotational symmetry
- order of rotational symmetry

Worked example

- Trace the equilateral triangle.
- Keep the tracing paper on top of the shape and rotate the tracing paper until it covers the original shape exactly.
- Keep rotating the tracing paper until it has made a full turn.
- How many times did the tracing of the shape cover the original shape exactly in one full turn?
- This is called the order of rotational symmetry.

An equilateral triangle has rotational symmetry of order 3.

I Trace these shapes and rotate the tracing paper to find out if the shapes have rotational symmetry.

- Write the order of rotational symmetry for each shape.

a  b  c

2 Predict the order of rotational symmetry of each of these shapes.

  ● Draw and then trace each shape to test your prediction.

a regular hexagon   Prediction: ☐   Actual order: ☐

b regular octagon   Prediction: ☐   Actual order: ☐

c regular pentagon   Prediction: ☐   Actual order: ☐

 **Stretch zone**

Draw a different polygon with rotational symmetry.

Explore 1

Draw specific shapes

Draw the shapes in the table.

- You will need a ruler and protractor to draw the shapes.

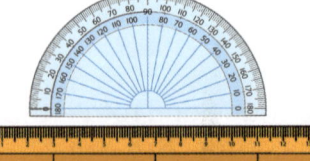

- Write at least three properties of each shape.

Shape	Drawing	Properties
1 Equilateral triangle with side length 2.5 cm		
2 Isosceles triangle with two angles of 35°		
3 Scalene triangle with one obtuse angle		
4 Rectangle with two sides of 3.5 cm		
5 Square with an area of 6.25 cm²		

9B Properties of 2D shapes

Explore 1 (continued)

Shape	Drawing	Properties
6 Parallelogram with one pair of angles of 55°		
7 Rhombus with sides of 3.5 cm		
8 Regular pentagon with a perimeter of 10 cm		
9 Irregular hexagon with one right angle and five obtuse angles		
10 Regular octagon with a perimeter of 12 cm		

Stretch zone

How many 2D shapes can you name that are not polygons? What properties must a shape have to be a polygon?

■ For more practice, go to Practice Book 6, page 126.

Explore 2

Draw shapes with rotational symmetry

Draw shapes with the correct order of rotational symmetry.

 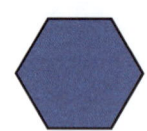  

Order 3
Order 4
Order 2
Infinite order of rotational symmetry
Order 1

You can draw more than one shape in each row if you like!

When we rotate a shape with order of rotational symmetry 1, it only looks exactly the same at the end of a full turn.

Stretch zone

What do you notice about the order of rotational symmetry of a regular shape?

■ For more practice, go to Practice Book 6, page 127.

9C Properties of 3D shapes

Discover

Build 3D shapes

Key words
- edge
- face
- vertex/vertices

Worked example

You can use modelling clay and straws to make models of 3D shapes.

Here is a cube and a model cube made from balls of modelling clay and straws.

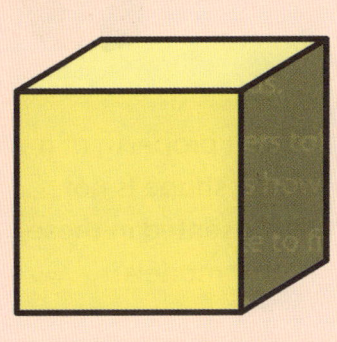

You need 8 balls of modelling clay and 12 straws to make a model of a cube.

I Make models of these shapes.

cuboid

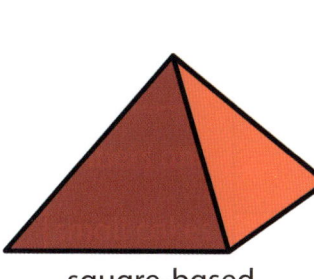

square-based pyramid

tetrahedron (triangular-based pyramid)

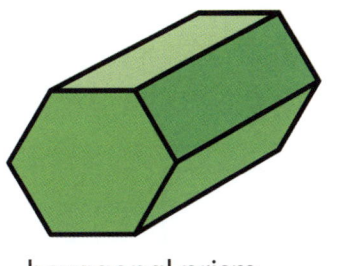

hexagonal prism

triangular prism

How many balls of modelling clay do you need to make each shape?

How many straws do you need?

Discover (continued)

2 In the table, write the number of balls of modelling clay and the number of straws that you used for each shape.

Shape	Number of balls of modelling clay	Number of straws
Cuboid		
Triangular prism		
Square-based pyramid		
Tetrahedron		
Hexagonal prism		

What property of a shape do the straws represent? What property do the balls of modelling clay represent?

What property of a 3D shape is not represented in these models?

3 Make two more 3D shapes of your own choice. Complete the last two rows of the table.

Stretch zone

Look at the shapes you have made. Can you see a relationship between the number of faces, vertices and edges? Describe any patterns that you notice.

■ For more practice, go to Practice Book 6, page 128.

Explore

Key words
- edge
- face
- vertex/vertices
- polyhedron

Classify 3D shapes

1 Complete this table to show the properties of each 3D shape.

2 Try to find an example of each shape. Write the name of the object in the final column of the table.

	Number of vertices	Number of edges	Number of faces	Object
Cuboid	8	12	6	a shoe box
Square-based pyramid				
Sphere				
Cone				
Cylinder				
Pentagonal prism				
Tetrahedron				
Octahedron				
Dodecahedron				

3 Write the names of these polyhedrons in a sequence. Each shape must share a property with the shape before and after it in the sequence.

_____

_____

_____

Triangular prism
Dodecahedron
Tetrahedron
Pentagonal prism
Square-based pyramid
Cuboid
Octahedron

Stretch zone

Use the shapes in **question 3**, and three more shapes of your choice, to make a loop. The last polyhedron must also share a property with the first shape.

9 Geometry – properties of shapes

159

■ For more practice, go to Practice Book 6, page 129.

Discover

Investigate nets

Think back

A net is a 2D shape you can fold up to make a 3D shape.
Here are some different nets of a cube.

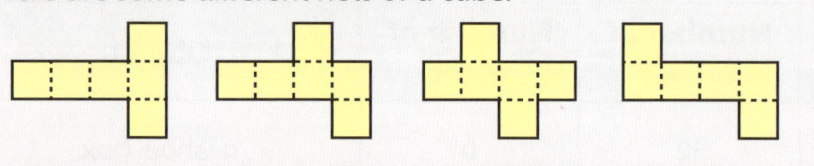

I What 3D shape do you think each of these nets will make?

- Write the name of the shape below its net.

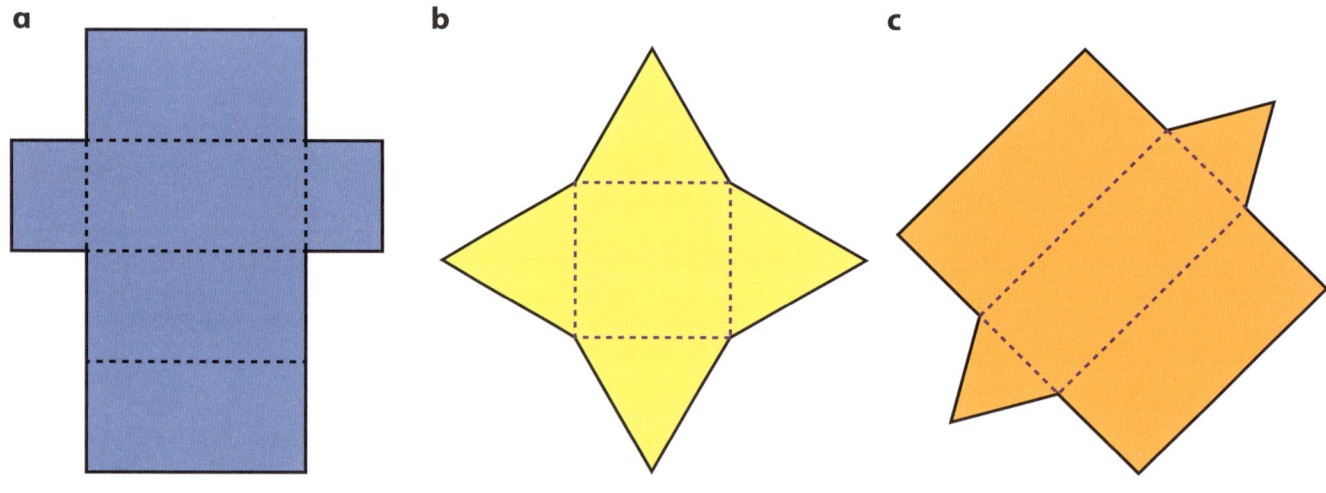

a

b

c

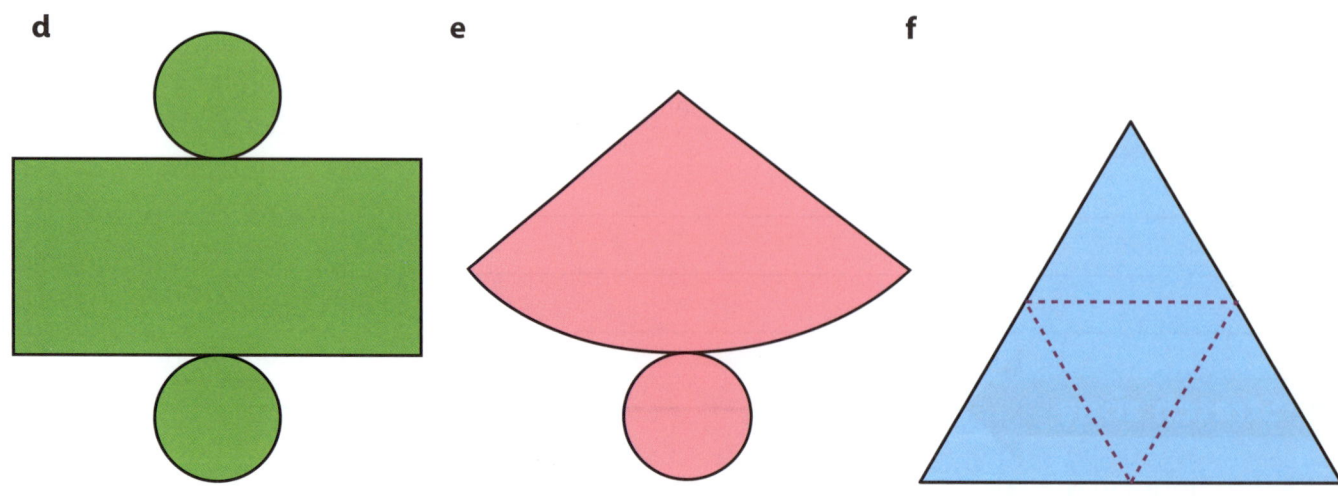

d

e

f

Discover (continued)

2 This net of a cube has been cut into two parts.

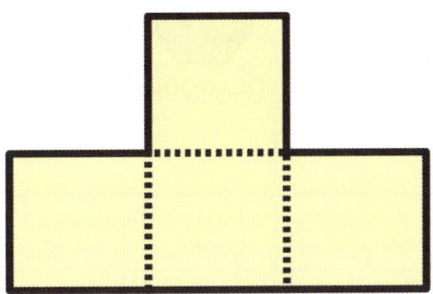 

There are lots of ways of joining these two parts together, but not all of them will fold to make a cube!

- Copy the two parts of the net on squared paper and cut them out.
- Use the two parts to make different nets of a cube.

3 Draw as many different nets of a cube as you can.

Discover (continued)

4 Find a box that is an interesting shape.

- Unfold the box so that you can see the net.
- Draw the net.

 oval  star 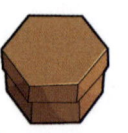 hexagon  heart

5 Make a scale model of your box so that the length, width and height of the new box are exactly half the size of those of the original box.

- Sketch the net of the scale model and write the dimensions.

 **Stretch zone**

Compare the volume of the scale model with the volume of the original box. What do you notice?

■ For more practice, go to Practice Book 6, page 130.

9D Making 2D representations of 3D shapes

Explore

Draw 3D models

Worked example

You can join four cubes together in different ways.

For example, you can make this model.

You can draw this model on isometric paper like this:

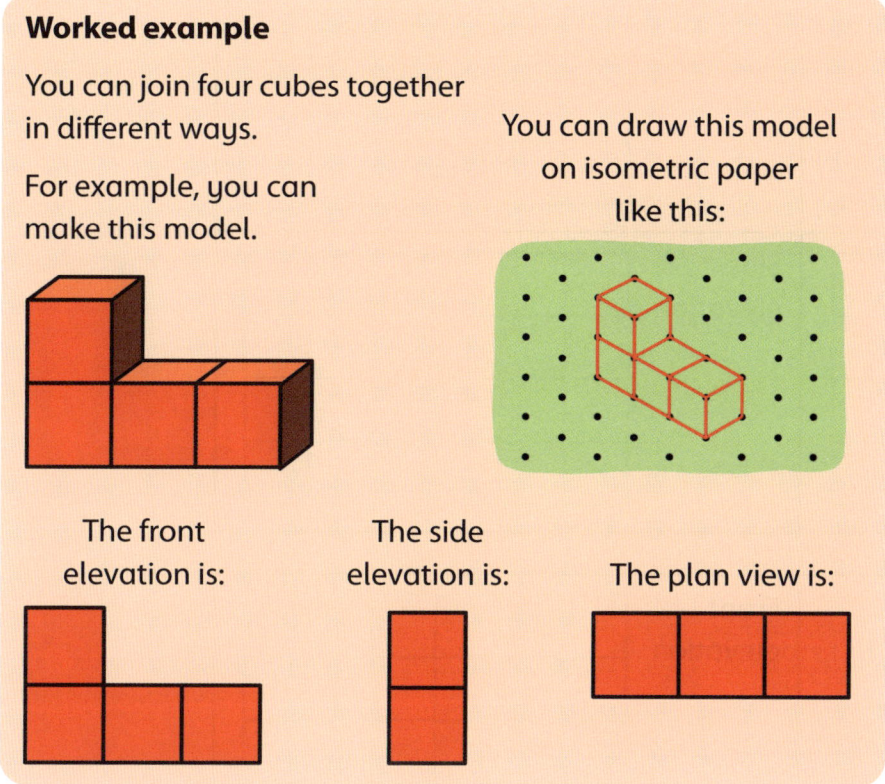

The front elevation is:

The side elevation is:

The plan view is:

I Use five cubes to make three different models.

- Draw the model on the isometric pattern below.
- Then draw the front and side elevations and the plan view of each model on the squared grids.

Model I

Front elevation

Plan

Side elevation

Explore (continued)

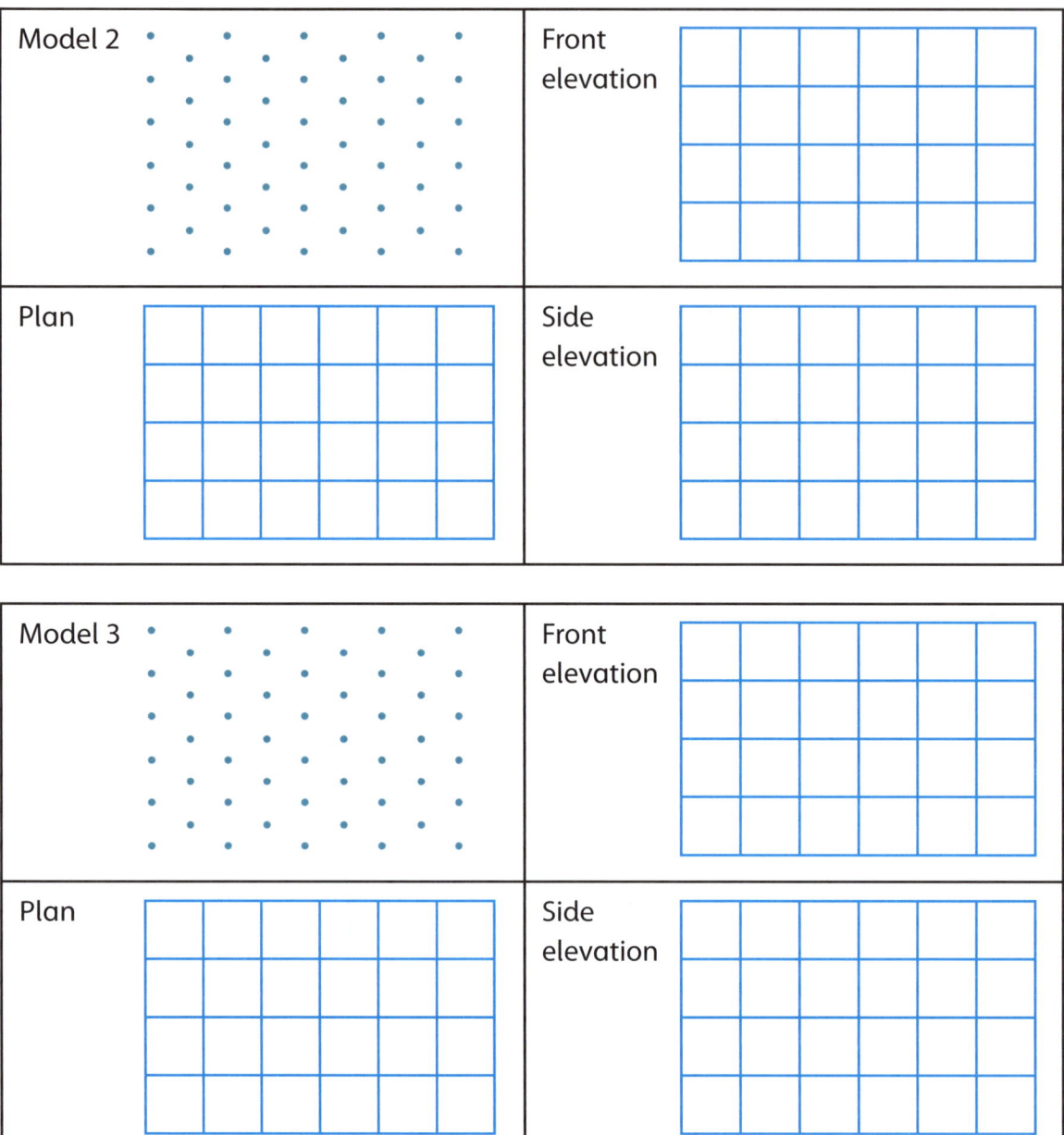

2 Swap your drawings with a partner and make each other's models.

Stretch zone

Investigate the different models that you can make using eight cubes. Choose one of your models and draw all the different views of your model.

■ For more practice, go to Practice Book 6, page 131.

9E Angles in shapes

Discover

Make and draw angles in shapes

Key words
- triangle
- quadrilateral
- polygon

Think back

An acute angle is less than 90°. An obuse angle is between 90° and 180°. A reflex angle is greater than 180°.

1 Make triangles, quadrilaterals and other polygons on your 9-peg circular pegboards.

- Draw your shapes on the pegboards below.

2 Label the acute angles 'a'. Label the obtuse angles 'o'. Label the reflex angles 'r'.

You can use a 9-peg circular pegboard and some elastic bands for this activity.

If you don't have a pegboard, you can just draw the shapes.

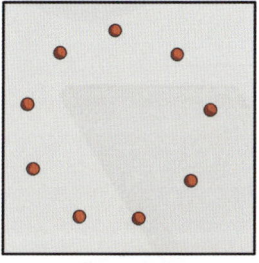 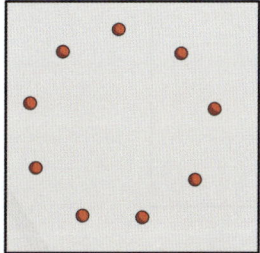 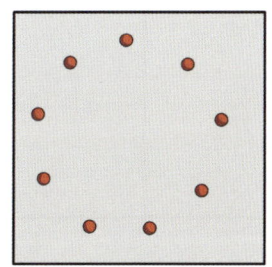

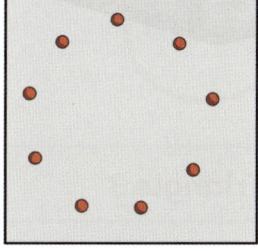 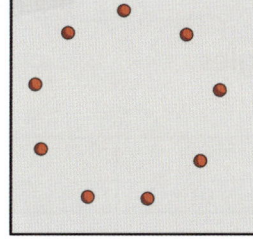 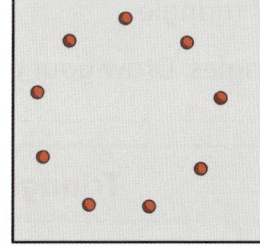

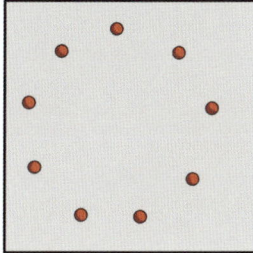 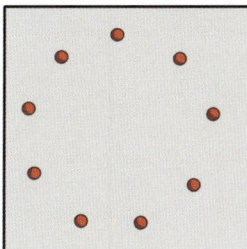 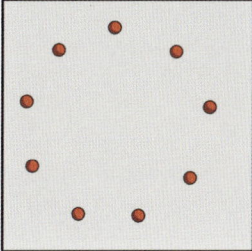

 3 Select three of the shapes and draw them accurately in your notebook. Label the length of each side and the size of each angle.

 **Stretch zone**

Draw a shape with at least one acute, one obtuse and one reflex angle.

165

9 Geometry – properties of shapes

■ For more practice, go to Practice Book 6, page 132.

Explore

Classify angles

1 Find three objects in your classroom. Each shape should contain a different type of angle: acute, obtuse and reflex.

- Sketch the objects and label the size of each angle.

Acute angle	Obtuse angle	Reflex angle

I found a reflex angle on the outside of my tablet.

2 Find three objects in your classroom that contain a triangle. Try to find three different types of triangle.

- Measure the angles of the triangles. Draw your triangles accurately.

Triangle 1	Triangle 2	Triangle 3

Stretch zone

True or false? You can create a tessellating pattern using any triangle.

■ For more practice, go to Practice Book 6, page 133.

9F Missing angles

Discover

Missing angles in triangles

Think back

> The internal angles in a triangle add up to 180°.

Key words
- missing angle
- protractor
- predict

Use the sum of angles in a triangle to work out angle c in each triangle.

Draw the four triangles below.

- You have been given two angles in each triangle.
- In each triangle, work out the size of angle c.
- Measure each angle c with a protractor to check your answers.

Triangle 1: angle $a = 65°$; angle $b = 75°$

angle $c =$ ☐ °

Triangle 2: angle $a = 24°$; angle $b = 66°$

angle $c =$ ☐ °

Triangle 3: angle $a = 115°$; angle $b = 30°$

angle $c =$ ☐ °

Triangle 4: angle $a = 58°$; angle $b = 58°$

angle $c =$ ☐ °

Stretch zone

Work out the area and perimeter of each of your triangles.

■ For more practice, go to Practice Book 6, page 134.

Explore

Angles in a pentagon

This irregular pentagon has been divided into triangles by connecting some of its internal angles.

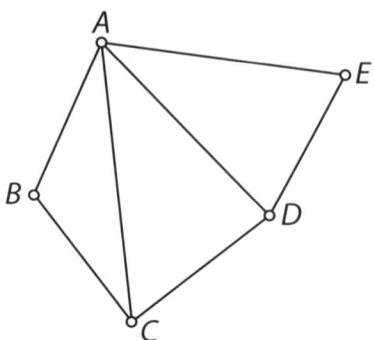

I Draw two different pentagons below.

- Divide each pentagon into three triangles.
- Measure and label the angles of each triangle.
- Add angles together to find the five internal angles of the pentagon (labelled A, B, C, D and E on this example).
- Add these five angles together.

Sum of the internal angles: [   ] °   Sum of the internal angles: [   ] °

2 What do you notice about the angle sums? Why do you think this happens?

_____

_____

Think about the sum of the internal angles in a triangle.

Stretch zone

Repeat this investigation with hexagons. Before you start, predict what the sum of all the internal angles of a hexagon will be.

■ For more practice, go to Practice Book 6, page 135.

9G Circles

Discover

Parts of a circle

The diagram shows three important words to describe parts of a circle.

1 Write a sentence to describe each word.

A radius is _____

_____

A diameter is _____

_____

A circumference is _____

_____

2 Use a pair of compasses to draw a circle with diameter 9 cm.

3 Draw and label the diameter.

4 Draw and label the radius.

■ For more practice, go to Practice Book 6, page 136.

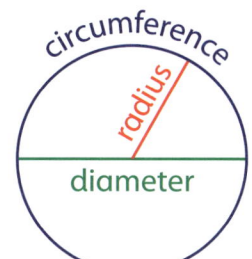

Key words
- centre
- diameter
- radius
- circumference

Talk to a partner to agree on your sentences before your write them.

Stretch zone

Draw two circles with a diameter of 5 cm inside a circle with a diameter of 10 cm.

9 Geometry – properties of shapes

169

9G Circles

Explore

Draw circles

Use a ruler and a pair of compasses to draw these circles.

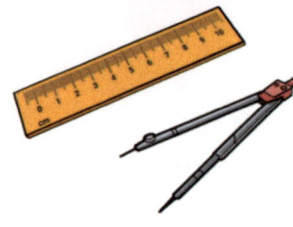

Key words
- diameter
- radius
- circle

1 A circle with a diameter of 7 cm

2 A circle with a radius of 3 cm

3 A circle with a diameter of 5.5 cm

4 A circle with a radius of 4.5 cm

 **Stretch zone**

Make a poster about circles. Research some more circle parts for your poster. What is the same and what is different about a chord and a diameter?

■ For more practice, go to Practice Book 6, page 137.

9 Geometry – properties of shapes

Connect

Design a playground

Work in a group.

You are going to design a new playground.

The playground needs a seesaw, a climbing frame, some swings and a hopscotch game.

Look at the photo. Can you see the different shapes and angles in this playground? Use this and other photos of playgrounds to help you.

Draw your playground design accurately and to scale on squared paper. Label all the angles and the lengths of the sides of each shape.

As a group, you must decide:

- the shapes you will use
- the angles you will use.

Your design must include at least:

- one regular 2D shape
- one irregular 2D shape
- two 3D shapes
- one acute angle
- one reflex angle
- two angles on a straight line.

What angles will you use to make the swings stable?

Stretch zone

Make a 3D scale model of the swings you designed for your playground.

9 Geometry – properties of shapes

Review

1 In the box, draw an isosceles triangle with:

   - a base length of 4 cm
   - two base angles of 30°.

2 Measure the length of the other two sides of your triangle Label the side length on the triangle. Calculate:

   a the perimeter of the triangle [ ] cm

   b the size of the third angle. [ ] °

3 Diego says, 'If you halve any obtuse angle you get an acute angle.' Is this true or false? Explain your answer.

   _____

   _____

4 This shape is called a frustum. Complete the properties of a frustum.

   Number of faces: [ ]

   Number of vertices: [ ]

   Number of edges: [ ]

5 Two angles of a triangle are 35° and 72°.

   a What is the size of the other angle? [ ] °

   b How do you know? _____

   _____

6 I draw a circle using a pair of compasses. The distance between the point on the compasses and the pencil is 3.5 cm.

   a What is the length of the radius of the circle? [ ] cm

   b What is the length of the diameter of the circle? [ ] cm

In this unit you will:

- draw, translate and reflect simple shapes on a coordinate grid
- describe position using all four quadrants on a coordinate grid.

? How can I describe the positions of objects on a coordinate grid?

Engage

Can you describe the pattern using coordinates?

What reflections can you see?

We can draw a coordinate grid on top of this pattern. This will help us to describe the pattern.

There are lots of repeating shapes in this pattern.

Discover

Key words
- coordinate grid
- quadrant
- origin

Use a coordinate grid

1 Draw a plan of your classroom on the coordinate grid.

- Use the origin (0,0) as the centre of the classroom.

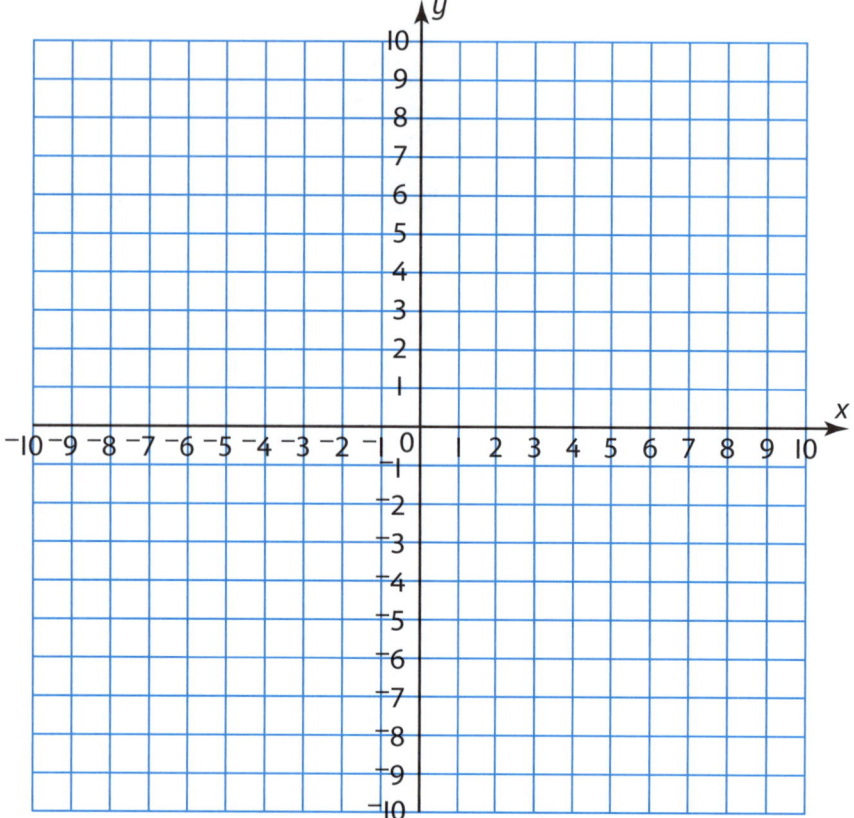

How can you find the centre of the classroom?

2 Write five statements about the positions of people or objects in your classroom.

- In your statements, use coordinates in all four **quadrants**.

a _____

b _____

c _____

d _____

e _____

In my classroom, Sohm is sitting at (⁻3,2) and one corner of the teacher's desk is at (0,5).

Stretch zone

Plot four different points that have the same x-coordinate and y-coordinate, for example, (2,2) and (⁻4,⁻4). What do you notice?

■ For more practice, go to Practice Book 6, page 139.

Explore

Draw shapes on a coordinate grid

1 Draw a different polygon on each coordinate grid. Each polygon must have at least one vertex in each quadrant.

- Label all the vertices of the shapes with their coordinates.

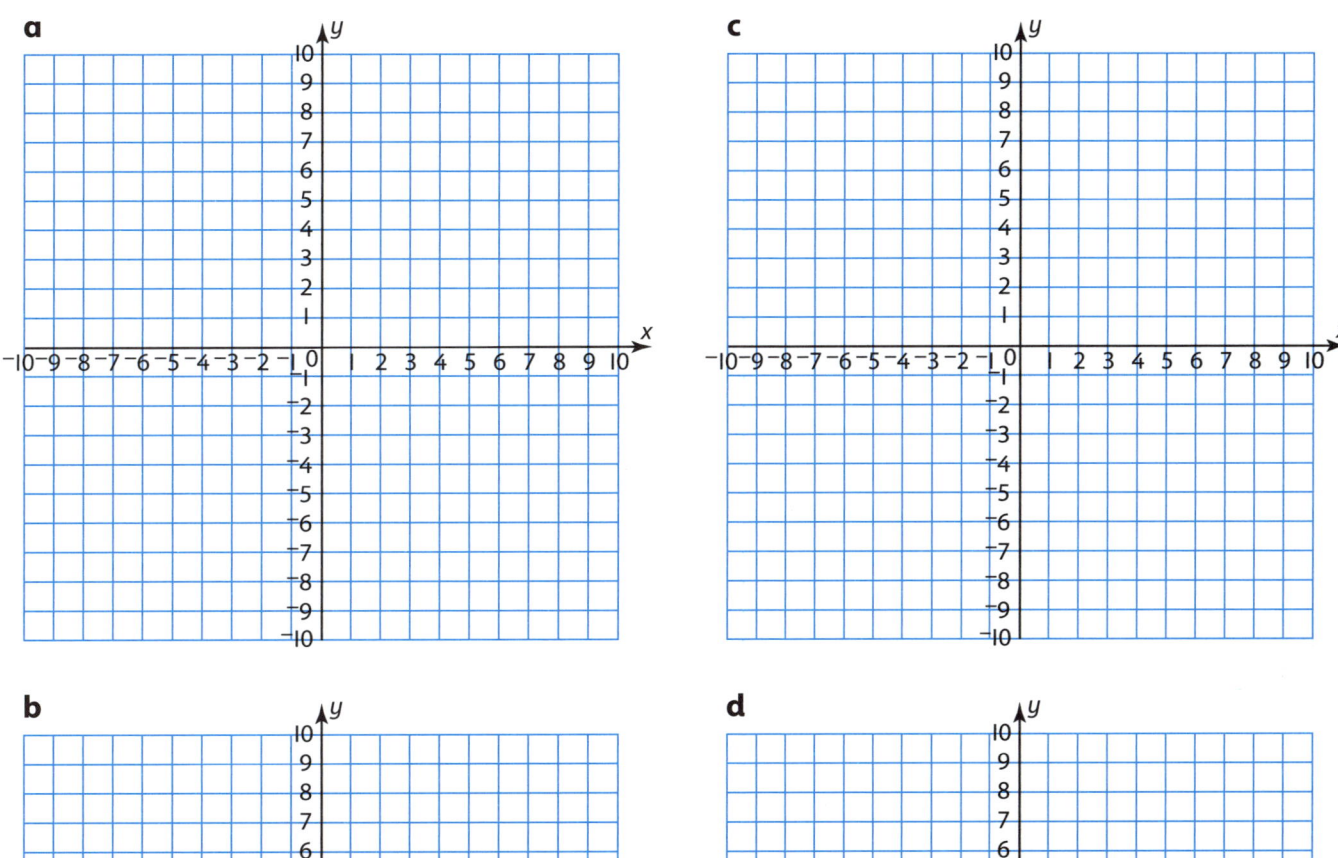

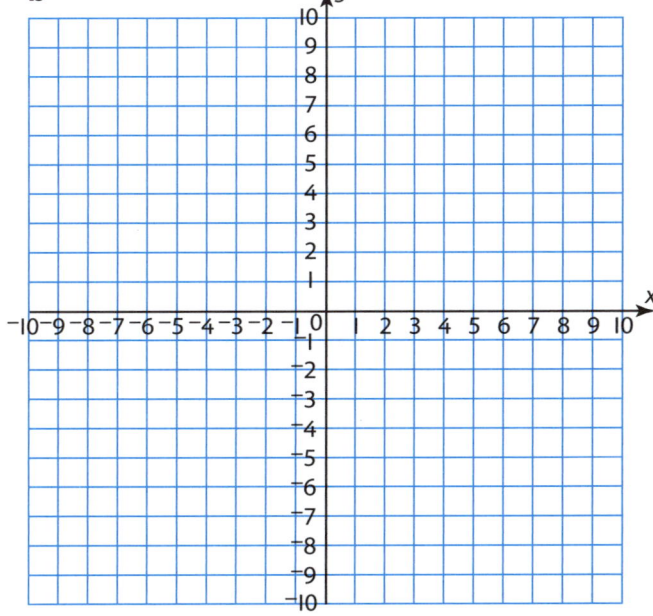

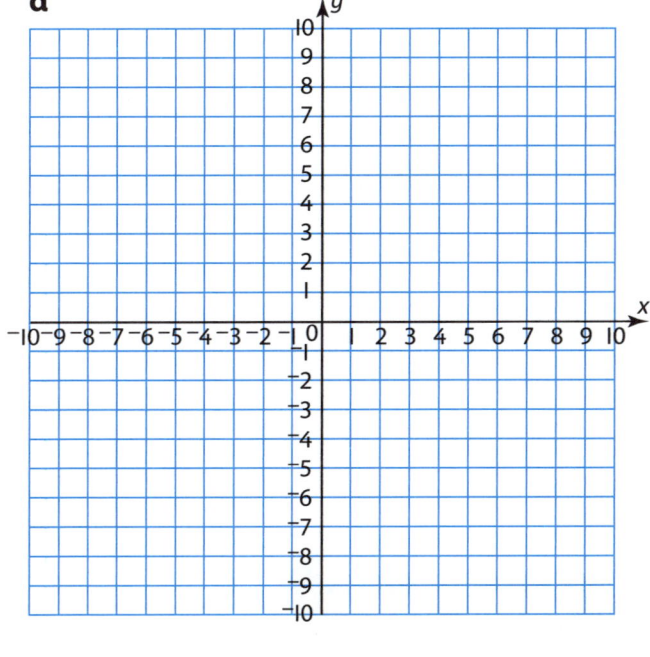

 2 Write the coordinates of the vertices of each shape in your notebook.

10 Geometry – position and direction

175

Explore (continued)

3 Swap the coordinates for your shapes from **question 1** with a partner.

- Use your partner's coordinates to draw their shapes on the grids below.

Write the name of the shape next to each shape.

a

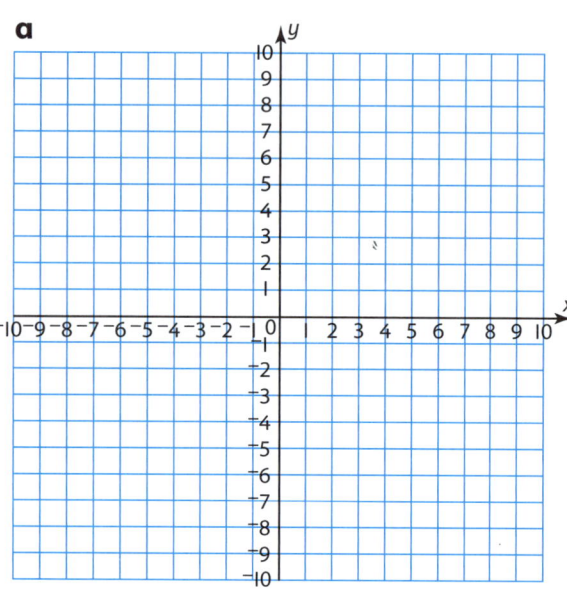

c

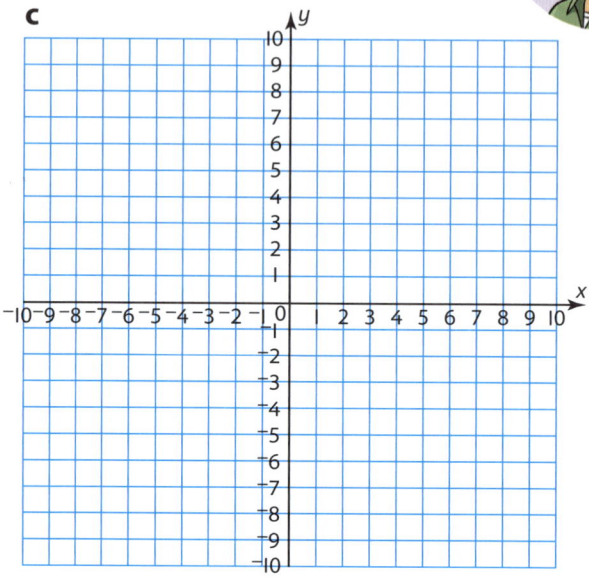

b

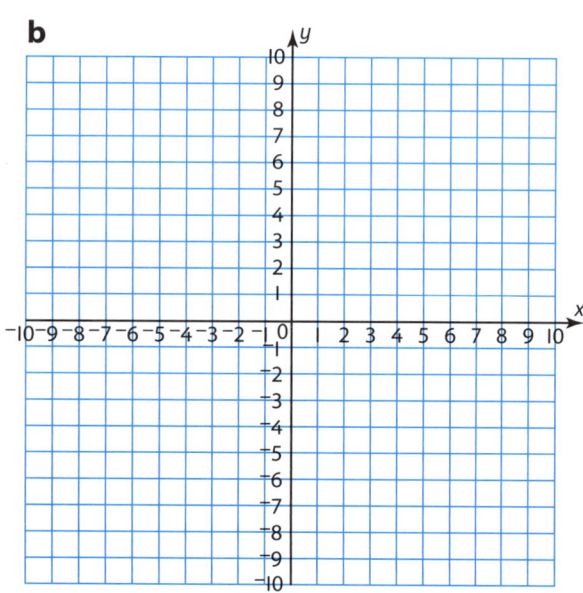

d

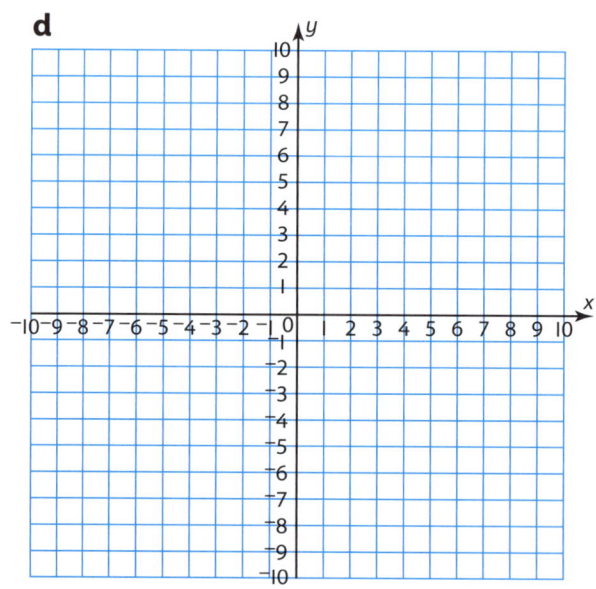

Stretch zone

On a coordinate grid, draw a square with one corner in each quadrant. What are the coordinates of the centre of the square?

■ For more practice, go to Practice Book 6, page 140.

10B Translations and reflections

Discover

Translate and reflect shapes in a pattern

Look at this piece of art.

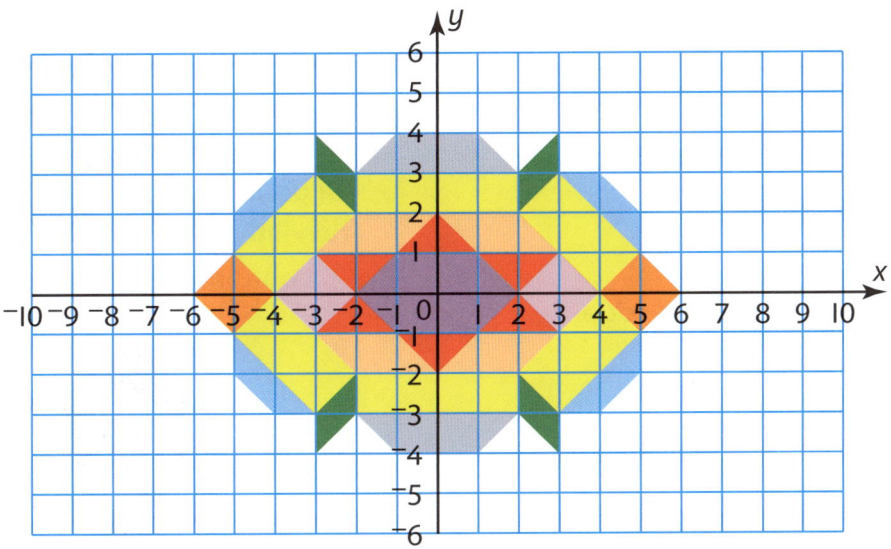

Key words
- coordinates
- axis
- translate
- slide

I chose one of the red triangles. The coordinates of its vertices are (⁻2,0) (⁻3,1) and (⁻1,1).

1 Choose three different shapes in this pattern. Write the coordinates of the vertices of each shape.

Shape 1: (☐ , ☐) (☐ , ☐) (☐ , ☐) (☐ , ☐)

Shape 2: (☐ , ☐) (☐ , ☐) (☐ , ☐) (☐ , ☐)

Shape 3: (☐ , ☐) (☐ , ☐) (☐ , ☐) (☐ , ☐)

2 Find one shape that is a translation or reflection of each of your shapes in **question 1**.

- Describe the translation or reflection, using some of these words: **up, down, left, right, *x*-axis, *y*-axis**.

Shape 1: _____

Shape 2: _____

Shape 3: _____

Stretch zone

Choose a shape in the pattern. Describe to a partner a translation that resulted in the shape. Ask your partner to tell you the position of the original shape.

■ For more practice, go to Practice Book 6, page 141.

10B Translations and reflections

Explore

Draw translations and reflections

1 Draw a simple shape on a piece of card. For example:

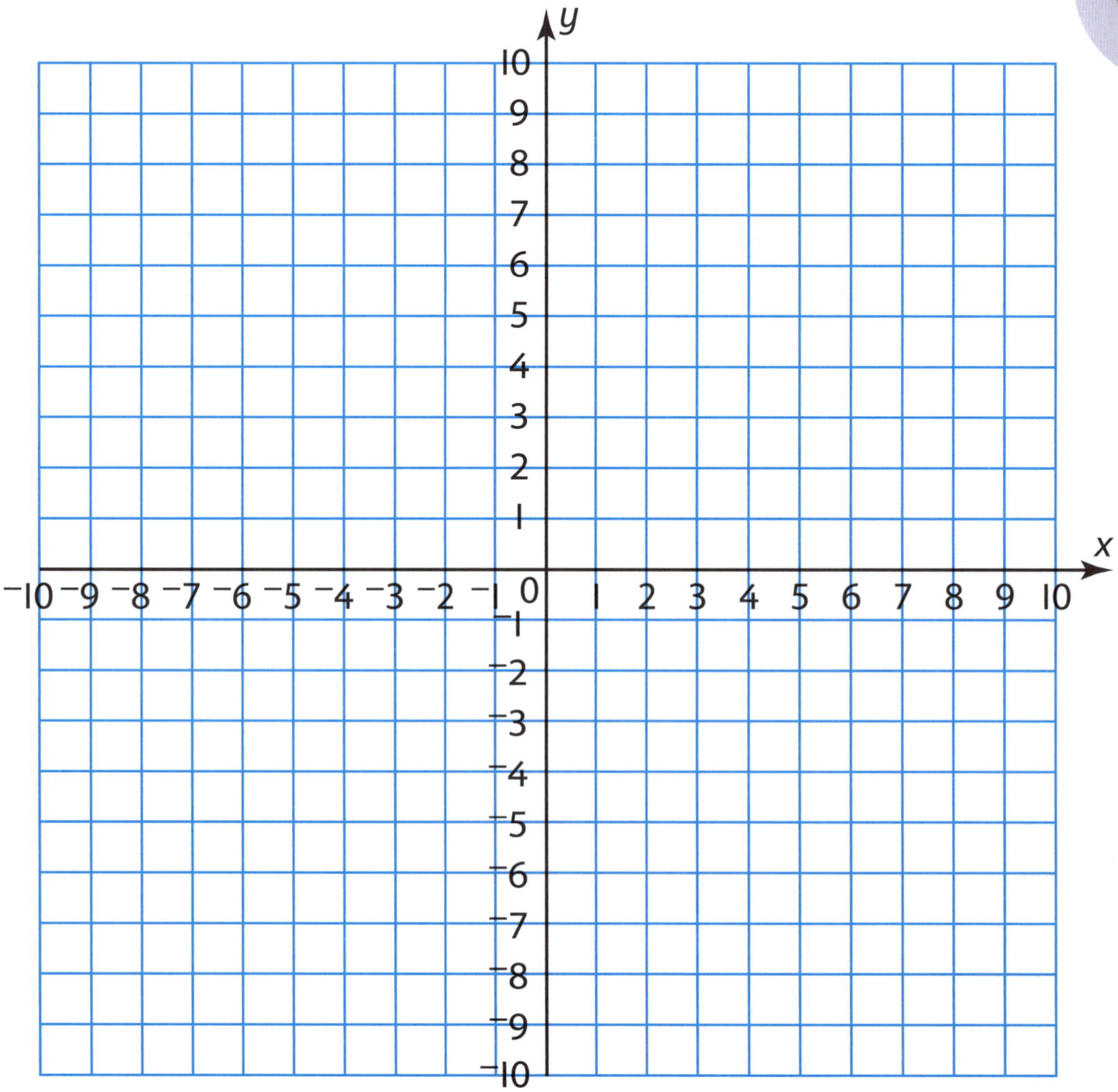

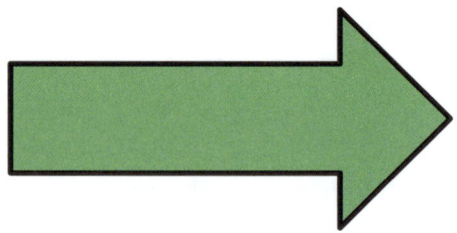

- Cut out your shape.
- Place your shape on the grid, with one straight edge against the *y*-axis.
- Then draw your shape on the grid.

Key words

- coordinates
- translate
- reflect
- slide

Position the vertices of your shape where two lines cross on the coordinate grid.

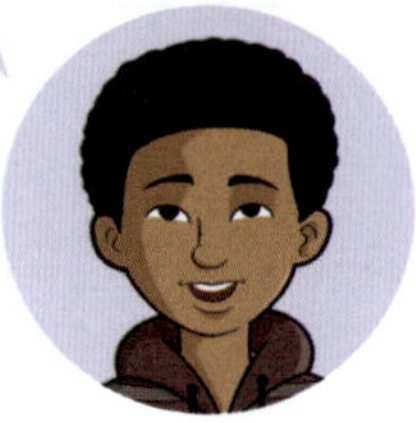

Explore (continued)

2 Write the coordinates of each vertex of your shape.

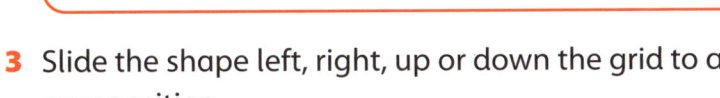

3 Slide the shape left, right, up or down the grid to a new position.

- Draw your shape in its new position on the grid. An example is shown below.

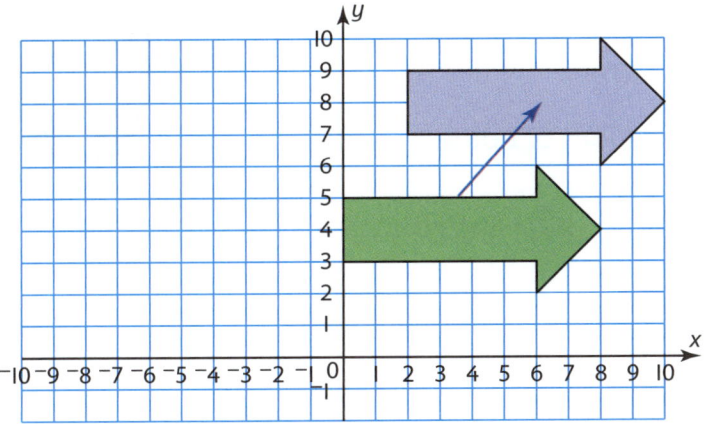

> I translated my shape up 4 squares and right 2 squares.

- Write the new coordinates of each vertex.

4 Reflect the original shape in the *x*-axis. Then translate the shape right 2 squares.

- Draw your shape in its new position on the grid. An example is shown here.
- Write the new coordinates of each vertex.

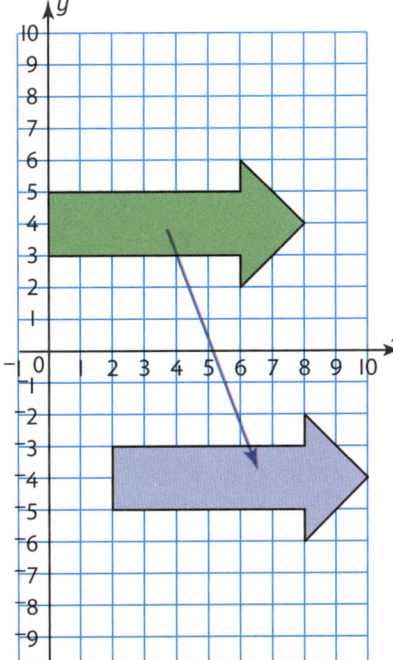

Stretch zone

Rotate the original shape clockwise through 90° about one vertex. Draw the shape in its new position. Write the new coordinates.

■ For more practice, go to Practice Book 6, page 142.

10 Geometry – position and direction

Connect

Logo design

1 Look at the logos below. Talk about them with your group. Can you see any translations and reflections?

What makes these logos memorable?

2 Design a logo for your school.

- Your logo should include translations or reflections or both.
- Draw your logo on the grid below.

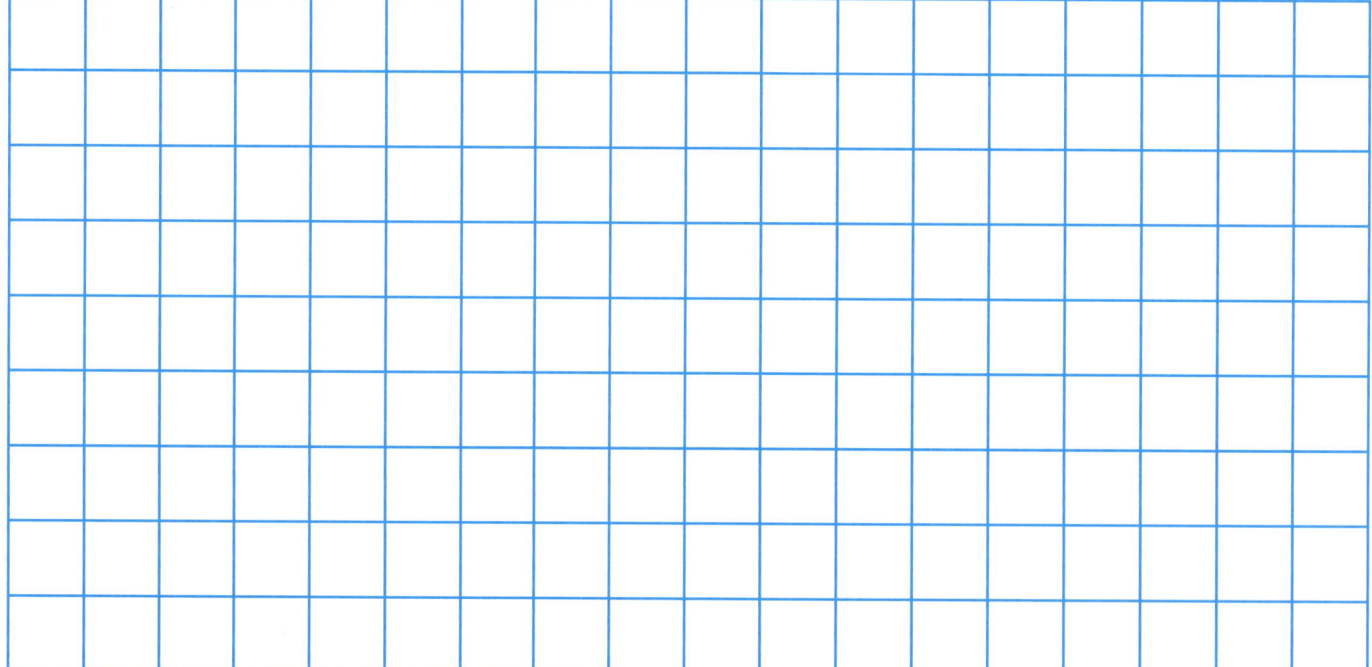

3 At the end of the lesson, vote to decide who has designed the best school logo!

Stretch zone

Use the internet to find some famous logos that include reflection, translation or rotation. Print your logos for a partner. Do they recognise any of the logos? Are some logos more recognisable than others? If so, why?

10 Geometry – position and direction

Review

1 Here is a quadrilateral on a coordinate grid.

- Translate the shape so that point A moves to point B.

- Draw the shape in its new position.

- Write the coordinates of the vertices of the translated shape.

(⬚ , ⬚) (⬚ , ⬚) (⬚ , ⬚) (⬚ , ⬚)

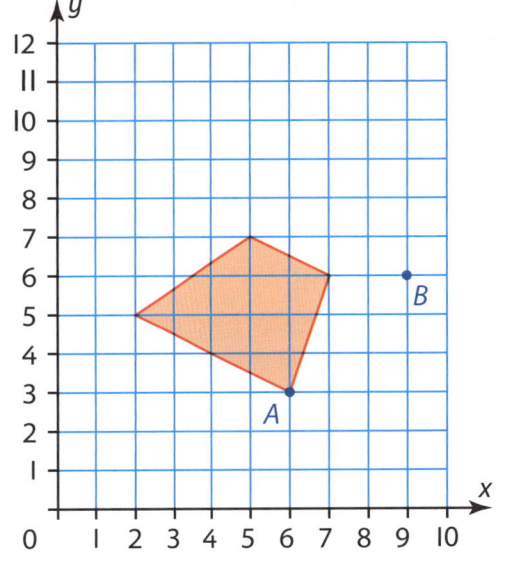

2 Plot a new point on this grid at position (–1,1). Join up the points to make a quadrilateral.

- Translate the shape 3 squares right and 2 squares up.

- Draw the shape in its new position.

- Write the coordinates of the vertices of the translated shape.

(⬚ , ⬚) (⬚ , ⬚) (⬚ , ⬚) (⬚ , ⬚)

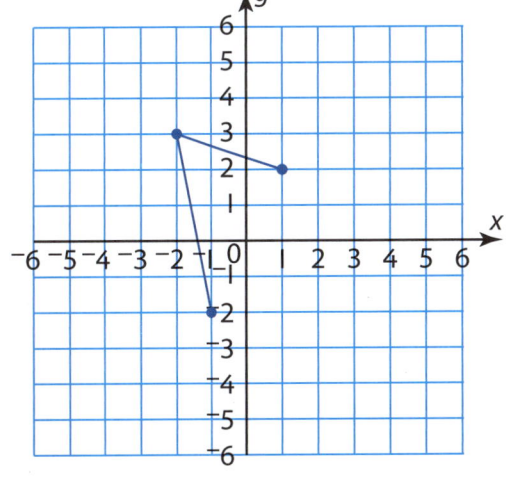

3 Look at this shape.

a Translate this shape so that point A moves to (3,3).

- Draw the shape in its new position.

b Reflect the original shape in the y-axis.

- Draw the shape in its new position.

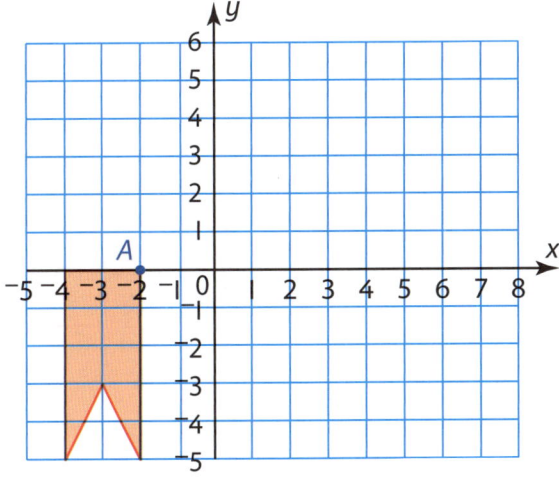

In this unit you will:

- calculate and interpret the mean as an average
- interpret and construct pie charts and line graphs to solve problems.

?

How can we find out the answers to some interesting questions and how can we present our findings?

Engage

What are some interesting questions we can ask?

When can we use a pie chart?

What is the climate in different countries?

What is the most popular activity to do in the school holidays? How can we find out?

How do the students travel to my school? Do students in other places use the same transport? How can we find out?

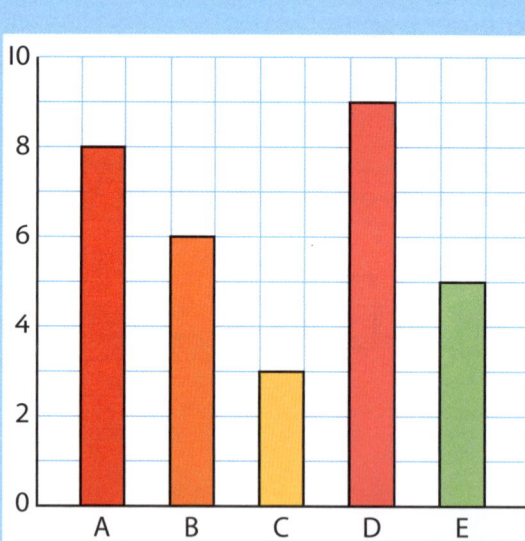

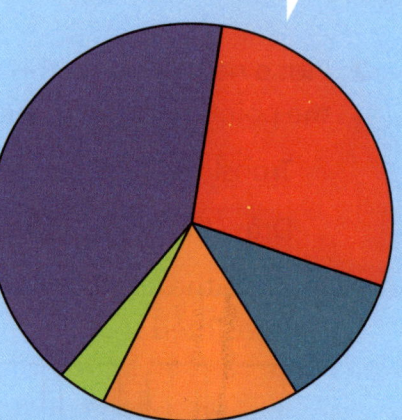

When is a Venn diagram useful?

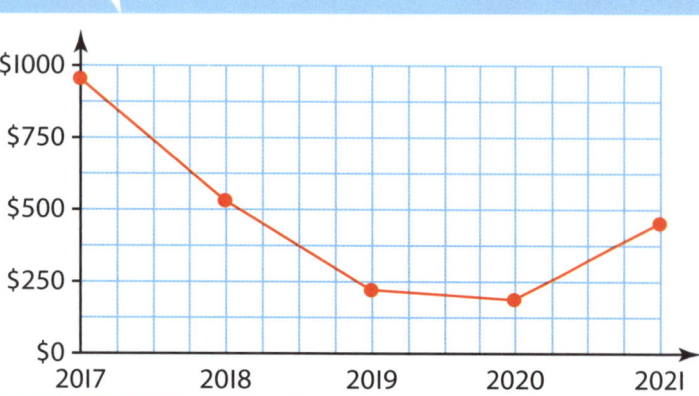

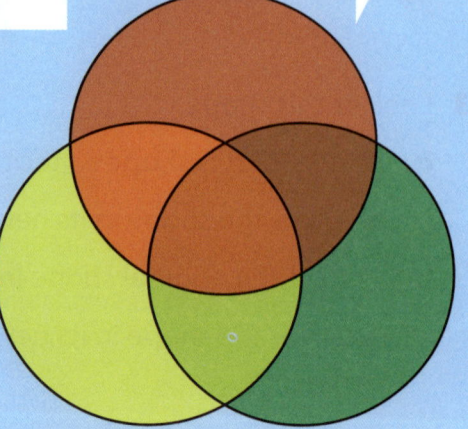

11A Averages

Discover

Calculate the mean

Key words
- average
- mean

1 Ask six classmates how long it takes them to get to school.

- Write the times, to the nearest minute, in the table below.

Classmate	1	2	3	4	5	6
Time (minutes)						

Why do we calculate the mean? What does it tell us?

2 a Predict whether your journey time to school is **longer** or **shorter** than the mean of your classmates' times.

My journey time is ⬚ minutes. I think my journey

time is _____ than the mean time.

b Calculate the mean time.

Mean time = (Total time) ⬚ ÷ 6 = ⬚ minutes

c Was your prediction correct? _____

3 Collect data for each question and calculate the mean.

a The mean number of minutes that ten of your classmates are allowed to use their phones each day.

Mean time = (Total time) ⬚ ÷ 10

= ⬚ minutes

b The mean number of siblings of ten of your classmates.

Mean number of siblings = (Total) ⬚ ÷ 10

= ⬚ siblings

Draw tables in your notebook to collect the data for these questions.

c The mean shoe size of eight of your classmates.

Mean shoe size = (Total) ⬚ ÷ 8 = size ⬚

Stretch zone

Repeat all the questions from this lesson, but use data for the whole class. What is the same and what is different about the results?

■ For more practice, go to Practice Book 6, page 144.

11A Averages

Explore

Mean sprint times

Here are the results in the men's and women's 100 m races in the Olympics in the years 1976, 1996 and 2016. Find the mean finishing time in each race as a way of investigating this question: Are women's times getting closer to men's times in 100 m races?

Key words
- average
- mean

You can use a calculator for this investigation.

1976 Men

Rank	Athlete	Time (s)
1	Hasely Crawford	10.06
2	Don Quarrie	10.08
3	Valeriy Borzov	10.14
4	Harvey Glance	10.19

1976 Women

Rank	Athlete	Time (s)
1	Annegret Richter	11.08
2	Renate Stecher	11.13
3	Inge Helten	11.17
4	Raelene Boyle	11.23

1996 Men

Rank	Athlete	Time (s)
1	Donovan Bailey	9.84
2	Frank Fredericks	9.89
3	Ato Boldon	9.90
4	Dennis Mitchell	9.99

1996 Women

Rank	Athlete	Time (s)
1	Gail Devers	10.94
2	Merlene Ottey	10.94
3	Gwen Torrence	10.96
4	Chandra Sturrup	11.00

2016 Men

Rank	Athlete	Time (s)
1	Usain Bolt	9.81
2	Justin Gatlin	9.89
3	Andre De Grasse	9.91
4	Yohan Blake	9.93

2016 Women

Rank	Athlete	Time (s)
1	Elaine Thompson	10.71
2	Tori Bowie	10.83
3	S.-A. Fraser-Pryce	10.86
4	Marie-Josee Ta Lou	10.86

Stretch zone

Investigate the difference between the men's and women's times for the 400 m race. What did you find out?

■ For more practice, go to Practice Book 6, page 145.

11B Probability

Discover

Key word
- probability

The Great Horse Race game

Your teacher will explain the rules of this game.

⭕ Play the game in a group.

Which horse do you think will definitely not win? Explain your answer.

I Put a tick ✓ in the grid each time you move a horse.

Horse								Winning post
I								
2								
3								
4								
5								
6								
7								
8								
9								
10								
II								
12								

Do you think the game is fair or unfair?

2 You are going to play the game again. Which horse do you think will win? Explain your answer.

> **Stretch zone**
>
> What is the probability that horse number 5 will win?

■ For more practice, go to Practice Book 6, page 146.

11B Probability

Explore

Probability outcomes

I   Complete this table.

- Look at the example answers and the explanations below to help you.

Key words
- equally likely
- outcomes
- event

Chosen outcome	Equally likely outcomes	Number of possible chosen outcomes	Probability fraction	Probability percentage
Roll an even number on a 6-sided dice	1, 2, 3, 4, 5, 6 I can roll 1, 2, 3, 4, 5 or 6.	3 There are 3 even numbers (2, 4, 6).	$\frac{3}{6}$ or $\frac{1}{2}$ There are 3 chances out of 6.	50% $\frac{1}{2}$ is the same as 50%.
Roll an even total on two 6-sided dice				
Roll a number less than 4 on a 10-sided dice				
Pick a 7 or a 9 from a pack of number cards 1–20				
Pick a 1, 2 or 3 from a pack of number cards 1–20				

186

Explore (continued)

2 Write two events with each of the following probabilities.

a $\frac{1}{2}$

_____

_____

For an event to have a probability of $\frac{1}{2}$, there must be only two possible outcomes.

b 0 (impossible)

_____

_____

c $\frac{2}{5}$

_____

_____

d $\frac{1}{10}$

_____

_____

e 90%

_____

_____

90% is equivalent to the fraction $\frac{9}{10}$.
What events have a $\frac{9}{10}$ chance of happening?

f I (certain)

_____

_____

Stretch zone

How do probabilities allow you to predict what will happen in an experiment?

■ For more practice, go to Practice Book 6, page 147.

11C Handling data extended project

Activity 1

Define the question

The data handling cycle

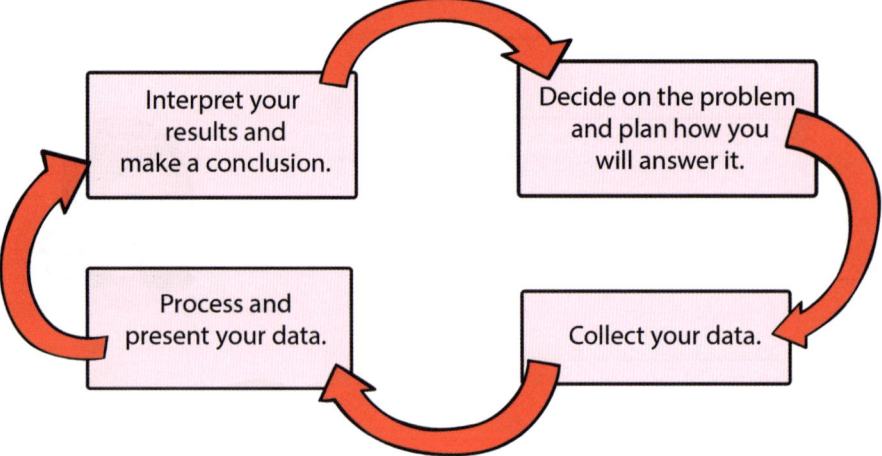

Interpret your results and make a conclusion.

Decide on the problem and plan how you will answer it.

Process and present your data.

Collect your data.

What would you like to find out?

I List all your ideas.

2 Choose one topic you are particularly interested in. You are going to research this topic in the next lesson.

Our topic is: _____

_____

Key words
- question
- data
- collect
- present
- interpret

I want to find out how we make school lunches both healthier and tastier.

I would like to know the best time of year to visit Switzerland.

I would like to find out what is a reasonable amount of time to spend at a screen each day.

■ For more practice, go to Practice Book 6, page 148.

11C Handling data extended project

Activity 2

Research the topic

Work in a group.

1 Complete this sentence.

The topic we are researching is _____

_____

2 Use the internet, newspapers and books to find information about your chosen topic.

Key words
- research
- data
- collect

We want to find out about school lunches. We will research what school lunches were like 50 years ago.

Source	Information we found out

11 Statistics

189

■ For more practice, go to Practice Book 6, page 149.

Activity 3

Carry out a survey

Key words
- survey
- collection
- question

Our survey topic is: _____

I These are the questions that we will ask people:

a _____

b _____

c _____

d _____

e _____

2 We will ask these groups of people.

Group	Number of people	Reason for asking this group of people

We are going to ask our lunchtime supervisors because they know a lot about our school lunches.

We are going to ask our grandparents because they know about school lunches 50 years ago.

 3 Record the results of your survey in a frequency table.

■ For more practice, go to Practice Book 6, page 150.

Activity 4

Present the data

I Choose one of your questions from **activity 3**. Decide how you will present your data. Choose either a pie chart or a line graph.

We chose a _____ because

_____

We chose not to use a _____ because

_____

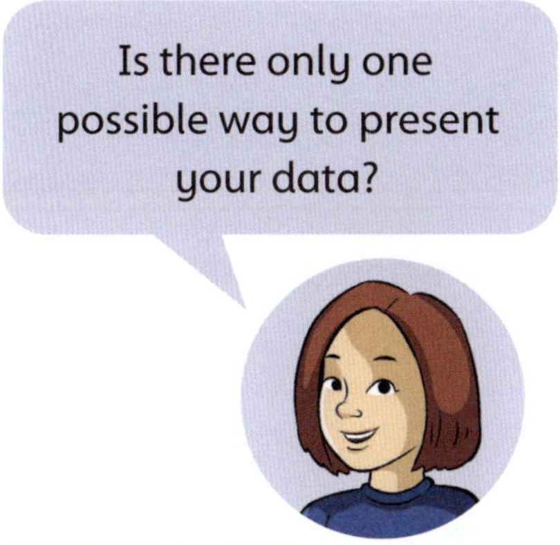

2 Draw your line graph or pie chart on the squared paper below.

Is there only one possible way to present your data?

11 Statistics

191

■ For more practice, go to Practice Book 6, page 151.

11 Statistics

Connect

Interpret the data and plan a presentation

Our topic was…

We wanted to find out about this topic because…

Our research showed us that…

We found out from our survey that…

Can you calculate the mean of any of your data? Does the mean help you to answer your survey question?

So, we now know that…

Stretch zone

Now that you have completed your survey, what further information would you like to find out? How will you find out the answer to this new question?

Review

1 This line graph shows the maximum temperature for five days.

What fraction of the days had a maximum temperature below 27.5 °C?

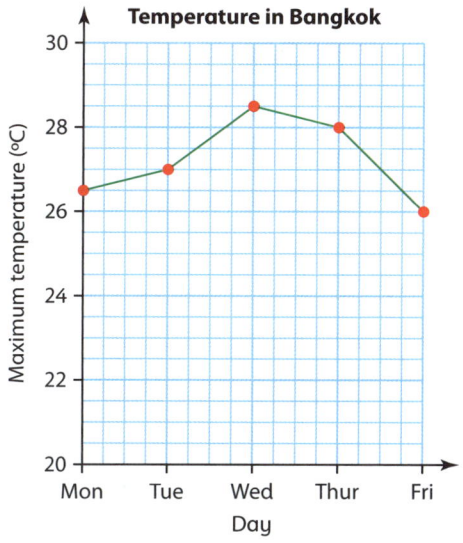

Temperature in Bangkok

2 This pictogram shows the number of cupcakes sold at a shop in one week.

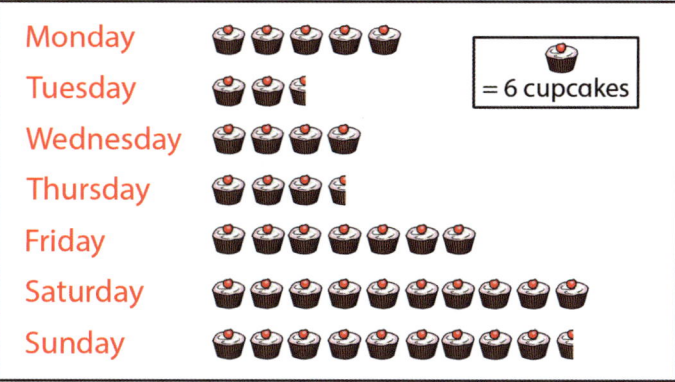

Monday	🧁🧁🧁🧁🧁
Tuesday	🧁🧁🧁
Wednesday	🧁🧁🧁🧁
Thursday	🧁🧁🧁
Friday	🧁🧁🧁🧁🧁🧁
Saturday	🧁🧁🧁🧁🧁🧁🧁
Sunday	🧁🧁🧁🧁🧁🧁🧁

🧁 = 6 cupcakes

a How many cupcakes were sold on Sunday?

b How many more cupcakes were sold on Friday than on Tuesday?

3 The pie chart shows the favourite fruits of a class of students.

a Which two fruits did equal numbers of students choose?

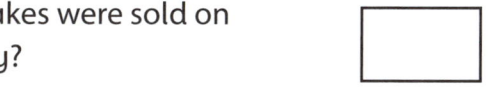 _____ and _____

Favourite fruit

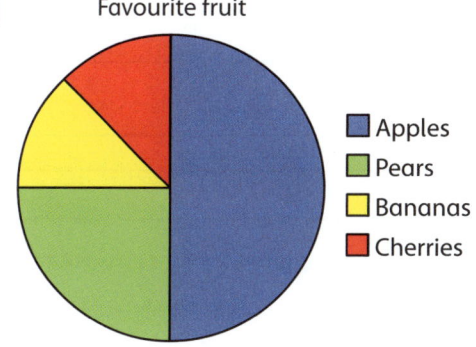

- 🟦 Apples
- 🟩 Pears
- 🟨 Bananas
- 🟥 Cherries

b There are 32 students in the class. How many students chose pears?

c How many more students chose apples than bananas?

4 This line graph shows the number of customers in a shop.

a What was the busiest time in the shop?

b How many more customers were there in the shop at 5 p.m. than at 10 a.m.

c At how many times in the day were there more than 10 customers in the shop?

5 Five numbers have a mean of 7. Four of the numbers are 5, 6, 8 and 8. What is the fifth number?

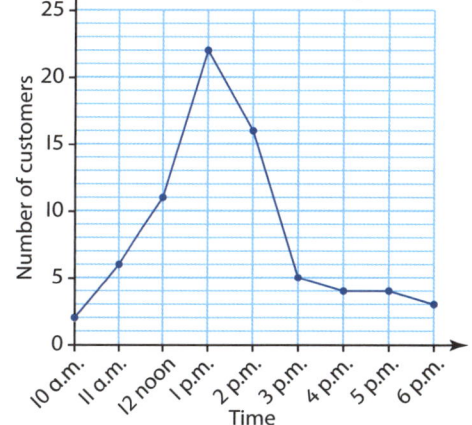

Customers in the shop

Glossary

algebra

_____

_____

_____

associative law

_____

_____

_____

$$14 \times 9$$
$$= (2 \times 7) \times 9$$
$$= 2 \times (7 \times 9)$$
$$= 2 \times 63 = 126$$

average

_____

_____

_____

Here are five numbers ranging from 3 to 9:

3   3   4   6   9

The **mean** is 5 because $\frac{3+3+4+6+9}{5} = 5$.

The **median** is 4 because it is the middle value.

The **mode** is 3 because it occurs most often.

BIDMAS

_____

_____

_____

B	( )	Brackets
I	x^y	Indices
D	÷	
	or	Divide and Multiply
M	×	
A	+	
	or	Add and Subtract
S	–	

BIDMAS helps us to remember the order of operations

brackets

_____

_____

_____

centilitre

_____

_____

_____

100 **centilitres** = 1 litre

100 cl = 1 ℓ

1 cl = 10 ml

1 centilitre = $\frac{1}{100}$ litre

circumference

_____

_____

_____

circumference

common denominator

_____

_____

_____

common factor

_____

_____

_____

common multiple

_____

_____

_____

12 is a **common multiple** of 3 and 4. It is also a common multiple of 6 and 2.

commutative law

_____

_____

_____

$12 \times 16 \times 5$

$= 12 \times 5 \times 16$

$= 60 \times 16$

$= 960$

composite number

_____

_____

_____

18 is a composite number because it can be written as 3×6 or 2×9.

constant

_____

_____

_____

conversion

_____

_____

_____

coordinate grid

_____

_____

_____

coordinates

_____

_____

_____

cross-section

_____

_____

_____

The **cross-section** of a cylinder is a circle

decade

_____

_____

_____

I **decade** = 10 years

10 **decades** = I century

decimal fraction

_____

_____

_____

decimal place

_____

_____

_____

degree of accuracy

_____

_____

_____

diameter

_____

_____

_____

This circle has a **diameter** of 7 cm

7 cm

distributive law

_____

_____

_____

46×8

$= (40 + 6) \times 8$

$= (40 \times 8) + (6 \times 8)$

$= 320 + 48 = 368$

dividend

_____

_____

_____

$$4\overline{)124}$$ with quotient 31

dividend

divisor

_____

_____

_____

divisor —— $4\overline{)124}$ with quotient 31

dodecahedron

_____

_____

_____

a regular **dodecahedron**

elevation (side elevation, front elevation)

_____

_____

_____

enlarge, enlargement

_____

_____

_____

equal chance (even chance, fifty-fifty chance)

_____

_____

_____

equally likely

_____

_____

_____

equation

_____

_____

_____

formula (*plural* formulae)

_____

_____

_____

inch (*plural* inches), foot (*plural* feet), yard

_____

_____

_____

12 inches = 1 foot
3 feet = 1 yard
1 yard = 36 inches
1 inch = 2.54 cm
1 foot = 30.48 cm
1 yard = 91.44 cm

integer

_____

_____

_____

interior angle

_____

_____

_____

interior angle

line graph

_____

_____

_____

This **line graph** shows the amount of rainfall each month

Rainfall (mm)

30
28
20 24 21
19
15
10
8
0
Jan Feb Mar Apr May Jun
Month

linear

_____

_____

_____

mean

_____

_____

_____

Here are five numbers ranging from 3 to 9:

3   3   4   6   9

The total is 25.

The **mean** is _____

millisecond

_____

_____

_____

mixed number

_____

_____

_____

net

_____

_____

_____

This **net** folds to make a cuboid

order of operations

_____

_____

_____

order of rotational symmetry

_____

_____

_____

ounce (oz) (_plural_ ounces), pound (lb)

_____

_____

_____

16 ounces = 1 pound

16 oz = 1 lb

1 ounce = 28.35 grams

1 lb = 453.59 g

1 kg = 2.2045 lb

parallelogram

_____

_____

_____

The arrowheads show which sides of the **parallelogram** are parallel to each other

percentage

_____

_____

_____

percentage increase, percentage decrease

_____

_____

_____

perimeter

_____

_____

_____

perpendicular height

_____

_____

_____

pie chart

_____

_____

_____

Favourite activities

Other 6% Golf 12%

Swimming 18%

Walking 40%

Cycling 24%

This **pie chart** shows the results of a survey about favourite sports

plan

_____

_____

_____

prime factor

_____

_____

_____

The factors of 24 are 1, 2, 3, 4, 6, 8, 12, 24.

The **prime factors** of 24 are 2 and 3.

prime number

_____

_____

_____

2, 3, 5, 7, 11, 13, 17, 19

These are the **prime numbers** less than 20

proper fraction

_____

_____

_____

proportion

_____

_____

_____

quadrant

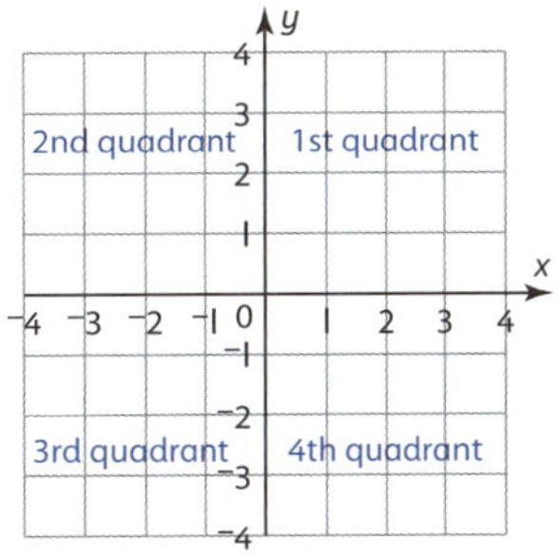

_____

_____

_____

This coordinate grid has four **quadrants**

quotient

_____

_____

_____

$$4\overline{)124} = 31 \text{ — quotient}$$

radius

_____

_____

_____

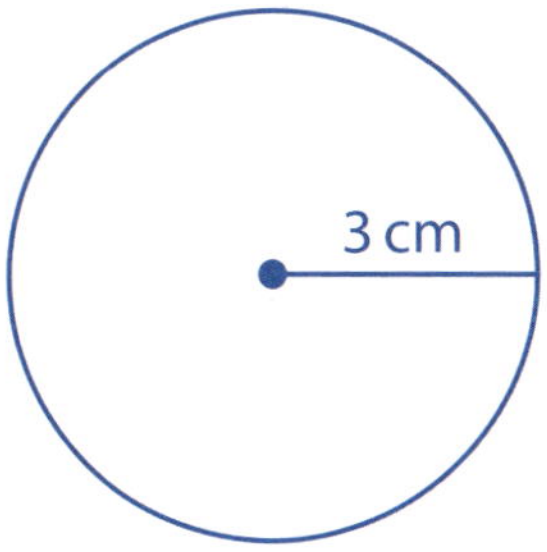

This circle has a **radius** of 3 cm

3 cm

ratio

_____

_____

_____

rectilinear

_____

_____

_____

rectilinear shapes

reflect, reflection

_____

_____

_____

The shape has been **reflected** in the mirror line

mirror line

reflex angle

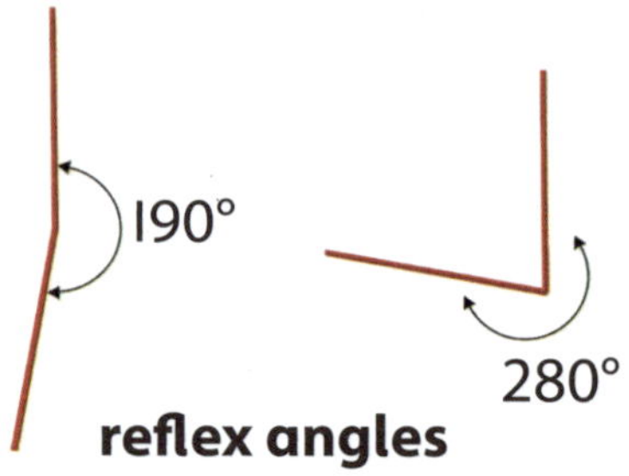

_____

_____

_____

190°

280°

reflex angles

rhombus

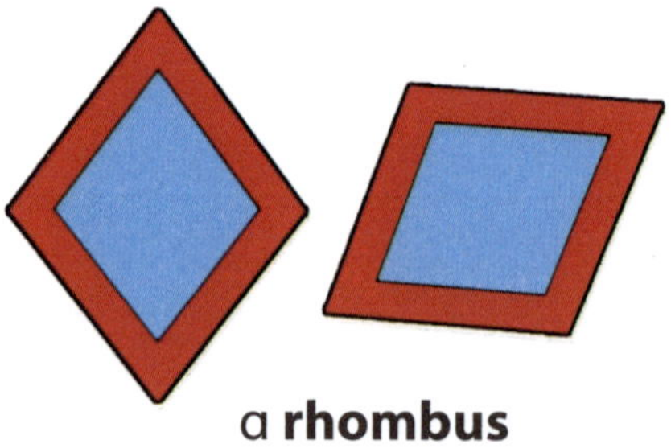

_____

_____

_____

a **rhombus**

rotational symmetry

_____

_____

_____

scale factor

_____

_____

_____

simplify

_____

_____

_____

symmetry

_____

_____

_____

A kite has reflective **symmetry** about a line

A parallelogram has rotational **symmetry** about a point

A cuboid has reflective **symmetry** about a plane

A pyramid has rotational **symmetry** about an axis

tangram

_____

_____

_____

a **tangram** puzzle

time zones

_____

_____

_____

11 a.m. New York

5 p.m. Rome

7 p.m. Moscow

tonne

_____

_____

_____

transformation

_____

_____

_____

translate, translation

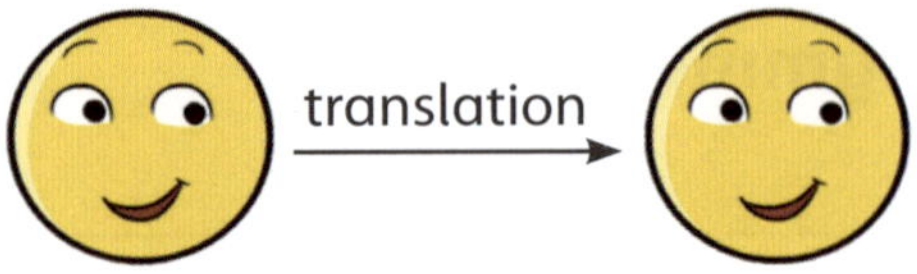

_____

_____

_____

translation

The shape has been **translated** to a new position

trapezium

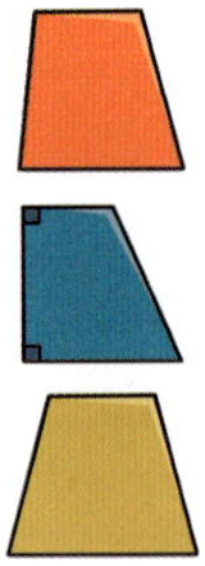

_____

_____

_____

trapezium

right-angled **trapezium**

isosceles **trapezium**

variable

_____

_____

_____

volume

_____

_____

_____